THE WORLD CRISIS
A World Wide Quest for a Sustainable Future
IT ALL STARTED WITH 9/11

ROY LUNN

the Peppertree Press
Sarasota, Florida

You can order this book at the following venues:
www.peppertreepublishing.com,
Barnes and Noble.com
Books A Million.com
as well as order directly through
the Peppertree Press by calling (941) 922-2662
and sending a check for $12.95 plus shipping and handling.

Copyright © Roy Lunn, 2009

All rights reserved. Published by *the* Peppertree Press, LLC.
the Peppertree Press and associated logos are trademarks of
the Peppertree Press, LLC.

No part of this publication may be reproduced, stored in a retrieval system, transmitted in any form or by any means, electronic, mechanical, photocopying, recording, or otherwise, without prior written permission
of the publisher and author/illustrator.
Graphic design by Rebecca Barbier

For information regarding permission,
call 941-922-2662 or contact us at our website:
www.peppertreepublishing.com or write to:
the Peppertree Press, LLC.
Attention: Publisher
1269 First Street, Suite 7
Sarasota, Florida 34236

ISBN: 978-1-936051-66-3

Library of Congress Number: 2009940621

Printed in the U.S.A.

Printed November 2009

Marlene & Tom,
 I think this might be the last book I write. On the other hand I have a few ideas ---

 Roy Lunn

Acknowledgments

I would like to thank the following people for their help in bringing this book to fruition, but also to add they are not necessarily in accord with the conclusions expressed.

Adolph Schmidt, for his continuing support, research, advice, basic editing and for all the long hours of reading and re-reading.

Dee Schmidt, for keeping the all important computer running and responding.

Nicola and Partice, my two daughters for spending many hours unraveling my engineers English,

Tom Bishop, whose quick response and magical touch kept me out of trouble.

Peppertree Press book publishing company for magically and painlessly transforming a rough manuscript into an attractively finished book and providing it with an expressively artistic cover.

My loving wife Jeanie, for providing encouragement and the much-needed piece and tranquility for many hours as I crouched over the computer while trying to help resolve the affairs of the world.

Many thanks.
Roy Lunn

CONTENTS

Contents
List of Illustrations and Graphs

Chapter 1	Preface	1
Chapter 2	About the Author	7
Chapter 3	Introduction	25
Chapter 4	Population	33
Chapter 5	Energy	45
Chapter 6	Environment	61
Chapter 7	What actually triggered the Recession?	75
Chapter 8	Management and Planning	83
Chapter 9	Sustainability	91
Chapter 10	The American Automotive Industry	97
Chapter 11	Future Transportation-Fuels and Vehicles	107
Chapter 12	Agriculture	133
Chapter 13	Education	145
Chapter 14	Governmental	153
Chapter 15	Humans-Body and Soul	175
Chapter 16	Summary	189
Chapter 17	Postscript	199

LIST OF ILLUSTRATIONS AND GRAPHS

page	fig	title
		Cartoon
10	Fig. 1	Reviewing designs in England with Henry Ford II
15	Fig. 2	Lunn and associates reviewing the Mustang I model
16	Fig. 3	Chevrolets-Duntov – Fords-Lunn
19	Fig. 4	"E" Car
34	Fig. 5	World Total Population
34	Fig. 6	Population 1950-2050
47	Fig. 7	Sun's Energy Spectrum
51	Fig. 8	World Energy Base vs. Generated Electricity Base
54	Fig. 9	Original Oil Endowment and Estimated Reserves
56	Fig. 10	World Oil Demand Balanced Against Supply
58	Fig. 11	Top ten countries by fuel usage
77	Fig. 12	Oil Price Escalation and the Effect on the Economy
111	Fig. 13	Basic Cars iO and Nano
126	Fig. 14	Big Red
128	Fig. 15	Lowered Trailer
130	Fig. 16	360 Degrees Rotatable Pods used in diesel electric shipping propulsion.
131	Fig. 17	Maltese Falcon sailing vessel

Published with permission. See Bizarro.com

Chapter 1
PREFACE

After choosing the subject for a new book, the author has to decide whether its message is to be based on imaginary situations or truth – fiction or non-fiction? If the book is to be written to sell and make money, the decision is usually fiction. This is because the general reader normally wants to be lifted into another imaginary world that provides thrills and entertainment beyond their every day existence. This is why the issues of sex, murder and intrigue are favorite subjects for many bestsellers. Readers can then hide themselves in exciting worlds of make-believe. However, the non-fiction author has to be a realist and portray situations as they are with real world analysis of problems and their possible solutions based on an honest review of facts. Very often this means reporting and discussing bad news which may be educational but is often depressing for the reader and certainly not pleasurable or entertaining. In addition, today, very few people involve themselves in serious reading with the ladies predominantly choosing fictional novels and the men mainly glancing though the local daily paper for headline news, the weather and maybe the market results. But, at least, everybody reads the tabloids in the checkout line at the supermarket. Also, with today's busy social activities, there is very little opportunity or desire for serious debate on the meaningful issues of the day, except when there is a major happening such as 9/11 or another war. This is because serious discussion takes time out from the wondrous life in which we are now involved, with all its pleasures and conveniences.

In the last 200 years the Western World has developed beyond belief to an exceptionally high standard of living. In the process the world changed from an agricultural to an industrial-based economy as a result of the Industrial Revolution. This was followed by a bewildering succession of inventions and achievements culminating in the communications era. So, today we live in wonderfully modern houses with all their comforts and conveniences provided by labor saving devices which maximize the time for relaxation and entertainment. Electrical equipment including TVs, computers and all manner of communication devices are as normal as is a car, or cars, in the garage, and everything is supported and maintained by a range of services including electricity, gas, telephone, cable and wireless internet, sewers, garbage collection, roads and general infrastructure, etc.

The move from an agricultural to an industrial based economy was also accompanied by a high degree of change from renewable to non-renewable materials- from a sustainable to non-sustainable existence. This, by definition, and in the course of time, would lead to the end of civilization. This situation has largely been caused by commercial developers employing readily available materials for short term gain without regard for their affect on the future. In addition, most of the non-renewables involved are obtained by mining, with all its land polluting problems. However, because in many cases these materials would not become exhausted for a considerable time, developers ignored the availability lifespan issue. This was reinforced by the general public because their reply regarding time outside their personal life span is, **"Why should I worry about it if I'm not going to be there when it happens?"**

This philosophy regarding development continued until recently when one of these non-renewable materials, oil, to which the world has become addicted, started to radically increase in price as a first sign of it becoming exhausted. This unplanned occurrence is also prior to evolving a renewable replacement. Therefore, because of its importance to the world's transportation system, oil, and its replacement, has become major factors in the world's economic downturn. Coincidentally, burning oil in internal combustion engines or in furnaces has finally been recognized as a major contributing factor in destroying the earth's atmosphere though pollution and in causing global warming.

Life developed on Earth about 200,000 years ago, and humans emerged as the dominant creatures and were blessed by Mother Nature which provided them with earth grown sun based nutrients for their sustenance. These consisted of Direct or Indirect recyclable sun based crops and ongoing Recyclable Systems i.e. air, water, solar, wind, hydro, geothermal, etc., all of which in turn naturally produced completely recyclable waste. Also, as is nature's way, it provided humans with ingenious digestive systems which have built-in check and balance systems which will only accept sun based products although in a wide range of diverse foods for supporting the multitude of complex body systems. This whole "Dust to Dust" sustainable cycle of events is known as **Nature's Way.** This is the total system of sustainability that existed and continued until a few hundred years ago when mankind discovered the easily available non-renewable materials which he could mine from the earth and use to improve his standard of living and generate profit. The World is still heading in this non-sustainable direction and is unwittingly leading us deeper and deeper into problems. Using large quantities of non-renewable mined materials for our existence is not only progressively demolishing the Earth's surface and poisoning the atmosphere, but it is also destroying the ongoing life supporting cycles of air, water, etc. which are fundamental to our very existence.

A little deep thinking quickly reveals that, if mankind is to survive into the future, all the materials man uses will have to progressively become renewable, and the only known way to obtain them, despite dreams of miracle devices, is by renewable crops and ongoing renewable cycles generated by the sun. This will naturally generate vicious competition for farmable land for growing them.

To solve the future energy issue, the academic fraternity has always dreamed of a little gadget that would magically extract hydrogen as a fuel from water in an acceptably efficient way. This hope remains a dream, and Nature's Way, which keeps all creatures alive, is the only practical known way to achieve the sustainability objective. Fortunately, one of the continuing energy sources is trees which have provided basic materials for mankind since the beginning of time. They have survived man's onslaught and with little help have been self perpetuating. Trees will continue as a principal material for many applications into the future because they, together with other vegetation, can also be used to generate such materials as Methanol. Methanol is not only a renewable substitute fuel for oil for use in internal combustion engines (ICE), it is also a potential source of power for the more efficient and cleaner fuel cell type of vehicles for the future.

Trees, because of their deep roots, are highly tolerant of drought and poor soil conditions. Apart from being a basic resource possibility to replace oil as a transportation fuel, trees will continue to be a principal material for building construction, furniture and a replacement for many other elements presently derived from oil. They are also one of the basic generators of the essential oxygen cycle and can provide positive modifying effects on the weather, including rain. Trees come in a variety of types to suit varying conditions and climates and produce a wide range of woods and other materials. Trees, therefore, in conjunction with other vegetation, are the principle key to expanding the world's agricultural system to provide man's needs for the future.

Until recently, this wondrous world that's been created for us was expected by many to continue ad infinitum. Now the world's deepening economic recession has interrupted this dream, and we are heading into further trouble. The seriousness of the situation has certainly grabbed everybody's attention, and people are now asking:

"What happened? I want my life back!"

This book tries to respond to this question by providing some non-fictional, realistic reading material as a basis for conversational debate on the subject. This includes the basics of understanding the fundamentals involved in sustainability and long-term planning and how they relate to "Nature's Way" of doing things.

Chapter 2
ABOUT THE AUTHOR

It's unusual to have a chapter about the author at the beginning of the book instead of the end, but many of his personal experiences dating back pre WWII were relevant to the automotive industry's history. It was also thought necessary to communicate the fact to the reader that Roy Lunn, although an amateur author with only three books to his credit, is however, a very experienced and skilled creator of innovative transportation vehicles over an extensive period of time. Also, it shows that his long and successful career qualifies him well to comment on the transportation industry's current situation and its future as well as on the very important decision-making on the renewable material to replace oil.

His involvement with the automotive industry started in England in 1939 when the storm clouds of World War II were rolling across Europe, and Mr. Neville Chamberlain was traveling backwards and forwards to Germany while making his abortive attempts to negotiate peace with Hitler. Roy Lunn was born in 1925 and started work in 1939 as a tool making apprentice at one of the small companies that were springing up in response to the pending war. He did this while still studying both aeronautical and mechanical engineering at Kingston Technical College now Kingston University, on the outskirts of London. Soon after WWII started in September 1939, the evening engineering classes at the college were changed to weekend classes to avoid the falling shrapnel that was being created at night by the anti aircraft guns responding to the bombing of London. This required working five days a week at the factory and attending classes on Saturdays and Sundays.

Roy's studies at the College included drafting and designing, and the small tool making company for whom he worked quickly took advantage of this capability. So he found himself at a young age being the tool designer and engineering representative as well as learning how to make the production tools. He continued this combination of work and college until 1944 when at 18 years of age he elected to join the RAF to train as a pilot although he had served as a naval cadet between 1936 and 1939. In 1945, when the end of the war in Europe was imminent, the RAF, because of his level of education, transferred him to the Royal Aircraft Establishment at Farnborough where he worked on the design development of gas generators for the first turbo-jet aircraft. He was discharged from the RAF at the end of 1945 and involved himself in freelance design on civilian projects until joining AC Cars of Thames Ditton in 1946. (This is the company that later built the Cobras for Carol Shelby) AC Cars was a small, high quality sports car maker with a history dating back to the early 1920's. In 1946 they were busily involved in designing and building their first post war vehicles which still had bodies made with wooden structures covered with hand made aluminum panels.

About the Author

In 1947 Lunn moved to another old, established sports car maker named Aston Martin which had combined with Lagonda cars under the David Brown Tractor banner. He became the assistant to Claude Hill, the Chief Designer. When Mr. Hill left the company, Roy found himself in charge of the DB2 program on which he had been working; he was to complete the design and oversee the building of the two race cars which he accompanied to France in 1949 for the first LeMans 24 hour race after the war. The DB2 was the car that later became famous in the James Bond movie, Gold Finger. This involvement with Aston Martin brought him into contact with another old English company which was looking for a new chief designer. At the ripe old age of 24, he found himself the Chief Designer of Jowett Cars in Yorkshire, England.

His first responsibility at Jowett's was to take over the continuing engineering of their newly launched Javelin model and to start work on the Jupiter sports car with Professor von Eberhaust, who had been contracted to design the chassis. Over a period of nearly 4 years, Roy Lunn designed a whole new CD (Commercial Mark D) range of utilitarian vehicles from one basic concept. This included: a family sedan car, a station wagon, a new type of crew cab pick-up truck and a new plastic bodied R4 sports car to replace the Jupiter. This turned out to be the first plastic bodied car. Roy headed up the engineering, building and testing of the prototypes of this range of vehicles in England, France, Switzerland and Italy from 1950 to 1953. Also during this time, he drove in competition as co-driver to Marcel Becquart, winning the RAC International rally in 1952.

While being interviewed by the BBC on TV about his plastic bodied car at the London motor show in 1953, he was observed by Sir Patrick Hennessy, the head of Ford of England. Sir Patrick was looking for an innovative engineer to start a Vehicle Research Establishment for Ford in Birmingham, England, and Roy Lunn looked like a good candidate. It should be noted that until this time all Ford cars produced in England had their concept design work coming from Detroit. Sir Patrick wanted to break this cycle and start creating models locally particularly suited to the European market. Roy Lunn was hired by Ford and assigned the task of gathering a team of engineers from British manufacturers, which were mainly centered in the Birmingham area.

Figure 1 : Reviewing the new concept designs with Henry Ford II

During this period, Henry Ford II took a personal interest in the project and visited the Birmingham facility to review progress. Figure 1 shows Lunn explaining the proposed designs to Henry Ford II and Sir Patrick Hennessy in 1954 at the Birmingham Research Station.

Lunn was also assigned the task of originating the design of the next Anglia model for production in England. These tasks were well under way by 1955 when Roy and two of his senior staff from Birmingham were sent to Detroit to review the design proposals with the Head Office. These proposals initially included a conventional driveline (Front engine, Rear drive.) and a Front Wheel Drive (FWD) approach. The FWD approach was totally new at this stage, but it was rumored that Morris would produce such a model in the immediate future. After review, the response from Detroit was most encouraging, but they preferred the conventional approach particularly as it would be the first product out of the new stable. Lunn returned to England and passed the conventional concept design to the production engineering group for processing. The car was designated the 105E model, and it went into high volume production in 1958. It became a main competitor in England to the Volkswagen Bug and was distinguished by its reverse angled back window. In recent years, it showed up again as the flying car in the Harry Potter's Chamber of Secrets, movie.

When Lunn returned to England, he became the Product Planning Manager for all passenger car models, and in 1956 Sir Patrick Hennessy directed him to make a presentation of the new car programs to the Ford of England Board of Directors at their Regent Street Office. Roy was impressed with the Dickens-like atmosphere of the London boardroom with its dark oak paneling, Victorian furniture and a huge grandfather clock. He was also impressed with the makeup of the board of directors who were all titled gentleman with either Sir or Lord in front of their names. When he started his presentation, he was immediately interrupted by one old gentleman, Lord Airedale, who asked Roy to say a few numbers so that he could adjust his hearing aid. This accomplished, Roy went on and made his presentation which was seemingly well received, and he ended with the usual invitation to ask questions. After a brief pause, one of the old gentlemen asked, "My boy, if this idea is so good, why hasn't someone thought of it before?" To Roy this was like being doused with a bucket of ice, particularly after experiencing the enthusiastic encouragement for new ideas he had received in Detroit. When he arrived home that night, his first words to his wife Jeanie were, "We are immigrating to America!" which they did with their two daughters in the summer of 1958 when he was listed in the London papers as another example of the "Brain Drain."

In 1958 when Lunn immigrated to the U.S., he was 33 years old, and his experience in design, product planning and holding executive positions in Europe between 1939 and 1958 had been a unique education in the automotive industry, particularly from the engineering and product planning point of view. The European manufacturers such as AC, Aston Martin and Jowett's, with their compact engineering teams, necessitated an individual's training to be on a broad basis, and, consequently, it was a wonderful arena to learn motor vehicle design. One had to become familiar with and be capable of designing and managing every component and system including the vehicle development. He then had to put it into production and at the same time use "judgment and anticipation" to create the right type of vehicle to suit the prevailing economic condition of the marketplace. This, of course, leads into the all important activity of product planning. It's also in contrast to the large manufacturers with their expansive engineering departments with many people performing specialized functions. The small companies that Lunn worked for i.e. AC, Aston Martin, Jowetts, etc. produced only a few expensive cars per week while at the other end of the spectrum, Ford of England dealt in the thousands of inexpensive vehicles per day.' He has always been thankful for the invaluable education that this range of experience gave him in a complex industry, particularly with regard to the basic car market.

When he arrived in the US, he was not sure which company he should attempt to join. He elected to stay with Ford because

About the Author

it was the one he knew, and they knew him. Also at that time, Ford USA was still going through its organization and product consolidation of the post war period. They had hired a team of top management away from GM; this team was given the label of the "Whiz kids." They included McPherson, of strut fame, as head of engineering and Robert McNamara as president of Ford Division who later became President John F. Kennedy's Secretary of Defense and Arjay Miller who became the first non-family member President of Ford Motor Company. Additionally, it was an exciting time when a handful of bright young executives such as Lee Iacocca were starting to influence the industry.

Lunn had to become familiar with the American industry and find his way around the Ford system and organization. The Ford engineering management in Detroit recognized this, and his first assignment was to the Ford Division Engineering as liaison with the Central Advanced Engineering Department where some of their projects originated.

After a few months on this assignment, he replaced the supervisor of the department who was leaving the company. He was then assigned the task of starting the Cardinal program. Even back in the late 1950's Ford USA gave consideration to building and marketing a small inexpensive car in the United States. Lunn's previous experience with small cars made him a natural choice for the project.

The vehicle his team designed was a basic 4-5 seater with a 1.5 Liter engine employing a front wheel drive transaxle configuration. After building two running prototypes using slave bodies, he recalls taking Robert McNamara for evaluation testing drives. This Cardinal design, which was Ford's first front wheel drive car, was never approved for production in the states, but it did become the basis for the 12 M. Taunus vehicle in Germany.

In 1960, Lunn became the head of the Ford Advanced Vehicle

Department and originated a whole string of projects including Big-Red, a massive truck for the new 42,000 miles of superhighway that was then under construction. (This truck is more fully defined in Chapter 14 of this book). His team also worked on designing and prototyping various vehicles, including a flying car. The flying car never got off the ground, but one of the sports cars became the Mustang I that was the experimental forerunner of the famous Mustang productions series of vehicles, and it was also the design basis for the Ford GT 40 racing car.

In the early 1960s, Life Science Library published a book titled The Engineer to portray the role of the engineer in industry. They chose Ford's Advanced Concepts Group as their introduction and described the group's activities under the heading **12,000 Engineers to Make a Car. The introduction stated:** The skills of the Ford Motor Company's 12,000 engineers were culled and coordinated by an executive engineer when it was decided to build a completely new car, the Mustang. In its deployment of battalions of engineers, the automotive industry is typical; no modern industry could function without a similar array of diverse technological disciplines.

Figure 2: Shows Executive Engineer Roy Lunn and some of his associates examining a model of the Mustang I.

The Ford GT 40 program originated in 1962 when Ford decided to re-enter the racing arena which at that time included stock and drag racing. They also decided they would like to compete in the highly sophisticated Grand Touring GT form of racing that at the time was dominated by Ferrari and involved long-distance events such as the 24 hour race at LeMans in France. Because of his previous experience in this field and being head of the Advanced Vehicle Department, he was invited into the subject discussions. It was originally decided that the quickest way to enter this field was to buy the present leader, Ferrari. To this end, Don Frey, Lee

ABOUT THE AUTHOR

Figure 2: Examining the Mustang I model.

Iacocca's right hand man, quickly organized a team of four, including Don Peterson, later a President of Ford, Bob Maguire from Styling, Phil Paradise, the Ford Manager in Italy and Roy Lunn set out to investigate buying the Italian Icon. The team returned to Dearborn to report that it was a favorable possibility. This resulted

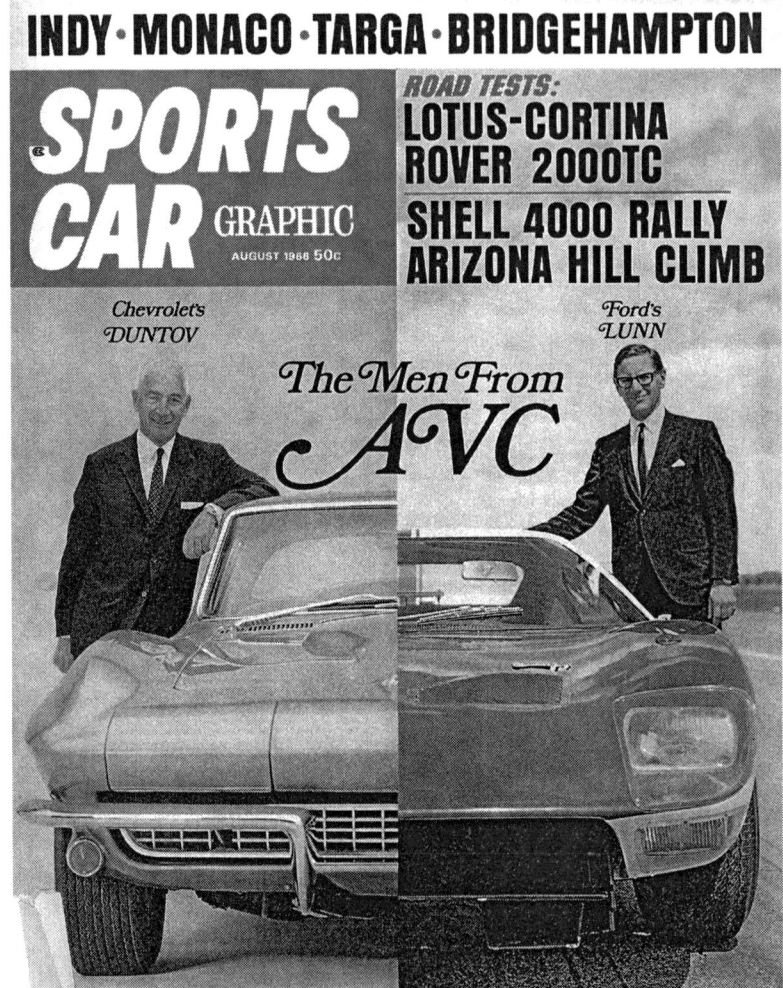

Figure 3: The Men from Advanced Vehicle Concepts.

in teams of lawyers and financial experts being deployed to Italy to finalize an arrangement. This exercise concluded with Ferrari backing out of the whole deal.

Back in Dearborn, Lunn philosophized that this was most probably a good outcome: If Ford had bought Ferrari and they had continued to win, it would still have been attributed to Ferrari's capability. However, if they had started to lose, it would've been attributed to Ford buying the outfit. He therefore proposed that Ford design and build their own car which would then be a true representation of their capability depending on whether they won or lost. This approach was approved, and Lunn was directed to develop a plan for accomplishing the task. His proposal was to initially set up a small central total engineering facility having access to all of Ford's engineering capabilities but operating with the freedom and flexibility of a small company. This was achieved by making an arrangement with Kar-Kraft in Dearborn and the Lola Car Company in England. A separate arrangement was made with Carroll Shelby to use his capabilities, team and facilities for developing and racing the vehicles. This approach was approved, and the first prototype was targeted to be running and racing within one year and hopefully winning after 3 years. This program resulted in winning the LeMans 24-hour race four times in 1966, 1967, 1968 and 1969 and Ford becoming the World GT Champions. This was accomplished initially with the GT 40 followed by the MK II and the MK IV designs. The MK IV was particularly interesting because it was totally designed and developed in the states with all American components and a glued together body and chassis structure. This vehicle won the Sebring 12 hour and LeMans 24-hour races in 1967. The team that performed this work is a good example of the "Skunk Works" approach with the department name of Advanced Vehicle Concepts. Figure 3 is a 1966 magazine cover showing the Author and his counterpart at GM, Zoro Duntov, who was responsible for the Corvette.

In 1970, American Motors was looking for a product innovator to initiate product programs for the Jeep Company they had just acquired. Lunn was always interested in a creative challenge and accepted this new task by becoming Jeep's Technical Director in 1971. Lunn's description of the situation was that it was the first time that he ever had to rise to zero. The products were outdated, the facilities were antiquated and the staff needed inspiration and direction. The first order of business was to update the CJ5 civilian version of the military Jeep and the Wagoneer Station wagon vehicle in order to keep the production lines running while totally new vehicles were being designed and developed. A CJ 7 model was created to replace the CJ 5, and the initial Cherokee model was derived from the old Wagoneer. Meanwhile, a completely new line of Cherokee light-weight, highly efficient utility vehicles were developed and became known as the first modern SUV class of transportation. These vehicles went into production in 1983, and nearly 3 million of them were produced over a period of 18 years. These basic utilitarian vehicles were uniquely designed for the purpose using a unitized body construction. They were light but tough and built to meet the tightening fuel requirements of the 1970s. They were unlike the competition that followed which were mainly derived from heavier trucks with their separate chassis design which made them much heavier and less fuel efficient.

In 1980 Lunn split off a small group to develop the Eagle which became America's first Four-Wheel-Drive car. It used an AMC Hornet car body and a completely new driveline developed by some of his old associates at the FF Developments Company in England and produced in America by the New Process Gear Company, a division of Chrysler Motors. The vehicle had all the comforts and conveniences of normal passenger vehicles but had the full-time traction capability of all four wheels without any input from the driver. It was light years apart from the part-time system used on the World War II military Jeep.

At the end of the 1970's, the second oil embargo prompted Lunn to generate another study of an efficient basic car that would achieve over 50 mpg. Again, he used the "Skunk Works" approach of a select group acting freely and expeditiously. They completed the design study which generated what was labeled the "E" Car to-

by permission of Sid Meade - artist

Figure 4 : The AMC-Renault 'E' Car.

gether with design layouts, seating buck and renderings. A picture of the 2 seat plus 2 car is shown in Figure 4 which emphasizes the "All Around" protection feature and the optional one wheel trailer that could be hooked on for additional passengers or luggage. He took copies of the design proposal to Paris for presentation to the Renault management who had acquired AMC. They were interested in the project but believed it was too advanced for that time.

As mentioned AMC had been purchased by the French company Renault in 1978 and, when Lunn had completed supporting the launch of the XJ Cherokee range of vehicles in 1983, he was nearing retirement age: So Renault asked him to become President of a new subsidiary named Renault Jeep Sport (RJS) to centralize their American competition activities for all vehicles that Renault and AMC were marketing in the states. This new company was located in Dearborn and was also charged with exploring new opportunities for corporate promotion. The first of these occurred in 1983 when the Sports Car Club of America (SCCA) approached

It All Started With 9/11

RJS with a request for an inexpensive racing car. They explained that racing had become overly expensive for the average amateur and what they really needed was a $10,000 vehicle. RJS replied that the only way to achieve this was to use an engine and driveline and a large percentage of the chassis parts of a production model but with a unique frame and body supplied in a kit form and with racing rules saying that no changes to the design or the components could be made. In other words, all the vehicles would be equal, and the drivers would be the predominant factor in the race. RJS built and shipped over 500 of these kits before donating the tools to SCCA to continue production. The car is known as the Spec Class of their entry level racing, and they are still available and appear at most SCCA events, but the price is no longer $10,000 after 26 years. They are delivered in a crate which contains a chassis with the engine and transmission installed and the unpainted fiberglass body mounted. The new owner has to assemble the chassis systems, such as the suspension and steering, and have the body painted together with its racing number, and he is ready for the track.

In 1983, the new XJ Cherokee was extremely well received in the marketplace, and it was decided to look at involving them in off-road racing both domestically and internationally, in the future. Internationally, the most challenging event is the Paris-Dakar Rally. The vehicles normally start in Paris early in the morning on New Year's Day and make their way down to the south of France. From there they travel by boat to Algiers where the race really starts. They then traverse some eight countries in North Africa which involves three weeks of off-road driving and living out in the open desert. The only problem was how to observe the event to gather data for designing a unique competitive vehicle. This was eventually accomplished by arranging for the Car and Driver Magazine to obtain two press entries for RJS in the 1984 Rally to enable them drive two specially prepared Cherokees to follow the rally and observe and learn about the vehicle design requirements necessary to compete in such an event.

Lunn organized the Paris-Dakar trip to include three professional drivers, a French-speaking employee from RJS and himself. The two specially prepared XJ new model Cherokees had inbuilt roll cages and, as they had to be self sufficient for long distances, 70 gallon fuel tanks and a variety of spares including wheels and tires together with heavy-duty suspensions, under shields, etc. They also had 20 gallon water tanks and stocks of food to last five people several days.

It was poetic justice for Roy Lunn, who had headed up the designing and developing of the production XJ Cherokee vehicle's, to be subjecting the results of his efforts to this extreme test of man and machine. The two vehicles successfully completed the journey to Dakar, and a great deal of knowledge was accumulated for future programs.

Lunn was deeply involved with the Society of Automotive Engineers (SAE) and over the years wrote and presented three papers:

- The Mustang Ford's experimental Sports Car. 1963
- The Ford GT Sports Car.1967
- AMC Four Wheel Drive Eagle.1980
  A New Dimension in Transportation.

He served as Chairman of the Technical Board in 1982-3 and was also a member of the SAE Board. He was elected a Fellow of the Society in 1983.

Lunn retired in October 1985 only to be called back to action one week later by the AM General Corp. This is the company that produces the military Hummer vehicle and had been sold by American Motors to LTV several years earlier. AMG had designed the Hummer as a general purpose vehicle to replace the original World War II Jeep, and they had already started production. Unfortunately, they had encountered a variety of product problems that were holding up acceptance by the Army, and they needed engineering help to resolve their difficulties. Roy Lunn joined the company as VP of engineering and stayed for a period of two years to oversee the corrective actions which allowed production to proceed, just in time for the desert wars. He retired again to his home in Florida in 1987 having spent some 48 years involved in the planning development and production of innovative transportation vehicles.

Throughout his long career in designing automobiles, the indiscriminate usage of oil and the question of what would eventually replace it became an ongoing personal concern of Roy Lunn. His position of heading up the Advanced Vehicle Department at Ford Motor Company in the 1950's could have given him the opportunity of investigating this all-important issue. He'd nurtured a long-term belief that the power embedded in a grain of corn or other recyclable vegetation was likely to be a possible source for a renewable replacement for oil. He had been interested in this possibility from the 1940s when he first heard about the frequent explosions in flour mills. When he brought up the subject with his scientific colleagues at Ford in the 1950's and 1960's, they convinced him that to propose spending talent and money on such a long term exploration at that time would be akin to committing career suicide because of the all powerful oil industry.

After he retired in 1987, he continued to follow developments through the media, internet, SAE and old industry connections, and he was pleased to see that work was proceeding on fuel cells and the likely fuel to power them included renewable crop-based materials. He was dismayed, however, when he saw these programs were being defused and confused by political and academic interference rather than assisted by the government and academia. When he heard that the whole subject of transportation energy was likely to be a major topic in the 2004 presidential election, he quickly composed a book on the subject entitled ***Oil Crisis: Sooner than you Think!*** which was published in 2003 and gave a forewarning of the oil situation that materialized in 2007-8. It also described the type of vehicle that would emerge and be suitable for the new fuel and a bad economic climate that was bound to exist. Unfortunately, the issue of oil was only given minor lip service in the 2004 election campaign, and the old, well-worn political pledge was again substituted "We have to free America of its dependence on foreign oil." Lunn therefore decided to compose another book titled ***Globalization: A Worldwide Quest for a Sustainable Future*** which was published in 2008. This book put the subject of a renewable oil replacement on a global basis because it permeates every crevice of modern human existence, and it is the first of the critical non-renewable materials to approach extinction. Both of these books warned of an economic downturn coincidental with an Oil Crisis.

This third book continues with the same theme of the importance of the transportation and oil issues and includes Lunn's first-hand observations of the automotive industry from prior to World War II until the present, together with suggestions for planning the future.

Chapter 3

INTRODUCTION

At this stage in the world's history it is fascinating, frightening and frustrating to view the present global situation of "Where are we?" and "Where we might be going?" Meanwhile, the so called more developed countries are now busily living in and enjoying this **Wondrous World of Comfort and Convenience** that has been created, and they unrealistically assume it will continue indefinitely. This high level of development of the modern world has largely evolved over the last 200 years by its human occupants exploiting commercially what was readily available to serve their short term needs, profit and pleasures without regard for its affect on their neighbors, their descendents or the future of the world in general. The whole situation has been exacerbated by the rate of development feeding on itself and accelerating at a high rate during this period. The international political arena had also been contaminated by hostile ethnic governments interjecting a toxic mix of politics and religion. The consequences of these actions or inactions are now showing up as a variety of horrendous global issues. Attempting to analyze these problems individually was quickly found to be impossible. It was found, however, that considering them in three general categories, **Population, Energy and Environment,** not only made their analysis feasible but also permitted the review and consideration of possible interrelated solutions.

Problem solving of multi international issues are nowadays classified under the heading of **Globalization** which is a newly found word, generated for the occasion. It has become the banner under which many pertinent current topics such as international trade and job exportation are discussed. This book, however, deals with the total time aspect of **Globalization and the World Crisis** by reaching back into history for information to aid decision-making on present and future issues which may extend into eternity. Short term decision-making without appropriate regard for the future is contrary to successful long term planning criteria which are based on **establishing the long term objectives and then making sure that, whenever possible, the multiplicity of short term actions are in keeping with that goal.** This planning beyond the human life span is fundamentally necessary but is entirely against human nature because many people refuse to think and debate into the future and deny logical conclusions with the response:

"Well, why should I worry? It won't happen in my lifetime."

It's difficult to get people to review problems and apply anticipation for long term planning by looking back from a point in the future that may be 50 or 100 years ahead.

They don't realize that framing ones thoughts and actions in unlimited time can make our short existence on earth more pleasurable and meaningful and be the basis of successful planning.

Introduction

The type and magnitude of the problems which the world now faces are beyond individual, industrial or market force response and have possible solutions only by united governmental involvement. This is unfortunate as politician's judgment and vision are often colored by their term of office, political implications and public opinion rather than solid knowledge, logic and scientific factors. The United Nations should be the organization to handle such situations, but at this stage, it has neither the established integrity nor the meaningful capability for handling such issues. Also, such unstructured meetings as the G8 and G20, the top 8 and 20 countries, are only intended to emphasize issues, not to resolve them. At this point in history there is a critical void in world governmental management capability and an appropriately structured and mandated organization for the international community to debate and resolve its mammoth issues.

The three categories of vital problems needing urgent global participation for their solution are all man made and caused by humans evolving into the world's dominant beings and making decisions without adequate thought and appropriate long term planning. These three categories follow.

Population

The present population of the world is approximately 6.5 billion, and it is estimated by the US Census Bureau to rise to over 9 billion by the year 2050. It should be noted that, essentially, all this increase will be in the less developed countries. Nature decreed that humans find great pleasure and enjoyment in copulating, and it becomes the sport and time-passer for unoccupied persons in these less developed areas where there's no other entertainment. This promiscuous situation produces disease and the birth of countless humans without preparing an appropriate sustaining environment for their existence. Basic education and aid to find occupational involvement will have to be developed, or there is a high risk of nature intervening with mass starvation and rampant disease. Migration of peoples from less developed to more developed areas is unavoidable and totally in keeping with human nature. Trying to strengthen borders by building walls will only be a temporary slowing down of the inevitable.

Energy

The modern world was created with, and is largely maintained by, a variety of energy resources. *Firstly:* There is the embedded energy that was locked into materials at the inception or creation of the world. These are non-replaceable and include all metals, chemicals, coal, gas, oil and other finite materials. *Secondly:* There is ongoing production and distribution of nutritional energy (food) that every human and living creature needs for its daily consumption. *Thirdly:* There is the ongoing need for energy or power for manufacturing and operating everything we use in our daily lives. This energy comes to us in the form of electricity, presently generated mostly by coal and oil. *Fourthly:* There is the special category of oil fuel energy to drive the transportation systems. This includes everything from personal cars to commercial vehicles which are the vital transporters of materials and produce. Then there is also shipping and air transportation which have played a vital role in speeding up physical world interaction.

The most urgent priority in these categories is developing a replacement for oil. This is a finite resource that has been indiscriminately squandered, and the demand for it is now starting to exceed supply and for which there is no proven or viable agreed replacement at this time. If this situation worsens, it will send the world further into economic, political and social chaos. Conversely, choosing a successful replacement for oil, from recyclable crop materials, will not only resolve the critical transportation problem but also many of the environmental issues. It will also provide an agricultural employment base for the less developed countries and be the key to solving many of the world's political issues. Oil happens to be the first of the critical non-renewable materials to reach a world supply crisis. In the course of time all other finite based materials will reach a similar point, and many of them, i.e. iron and cement and all metals, are already showing the initial indicators of undue price escalation even though they may not be extinct for hundreds of years.

Environmental

As stated, over the last 200 years the developing world has changed radically from an agricultural to an industrialized basis. This radical change, aimed at improving man's material wealth, has brought with it massive negatives affecting the world's environment. These include: deforestation and degradation of the earth's surface by mining of "one time only available" mineral and fossil resources, killing many of the biological ingredients in the soil by chemical farming usage, pollution of the atmosphere by generating toxic gases and by poisoning the earth and oceans by burying and dumping waste byproducts in the hopes that the mighty planet will absorb them. These negatives continued to increase with the world's ever escalating population and rate of development. It is now necessary to enact ways of reducing these negatives and to start the long process of cleaning up the degradation that has already occurred in addition to finding or generating renewable non-polluting materials as replacements which are all likely to be derived from agricultural sources.

Until a few hundred years ago the world and human evolution

was on a path of sustainability. The short term desire to increase GDP (Gross Domestic Product) and making money has led the world in the dangerous direction of a non-sustainable existence. It is now necessary to progressively substitute all necessary non-renewable with renewable materials, starting with oil. This will initiate a progressively ongoing battle for land usage among food, energy and all other materials that will have to be changed to a renewable base in order to achieve sustainability.

This book aims to review the three categories of challenging **World Crisis** issues in more detail together with their interactions and possible solutions on a **Globalization** basis.

Many people ask the question **"Do you agree or disagree with Globalization?"**

Globalization is not a question but an already accomplished and progressively ongoing factor that has been happening for many generations. Like the rotation of the earth, it is a factor that will continue to happen regardless of people's opinions.

Therefore, the only question remaining is: **Do you want to join in and help plan and guide its nature, or do you want to want to stand on the sidelines chanting objections to its inevitable ongoing existence and conclusions?"**

Chapter 4
POPULATION

It's remarkable to review the world's **Population Explosion** over the last 200 years. It took from the dawn of mankind until 1830 AD, over 12,000 years, for the world population of humans to grow from 6 million in 10,000 BC to a total of 1 billion. But it only took one hundred years to expand to the 2nd billion level; the 3rd billion was achieved in another 30 years; the 4th billion in fifteen years; the 5th in 12 years. By 1999 AD the level of the population had risen to 6 billion, and today it is estimated, by the U.S. Census Bureau, to be at 6.5 billion, and they project it will grow to over 9 billion by 2050 AD if left unchecked. This total world population growth is depicted in Figure 5:

A more detailed history of world population between 1950 AD and 2050 AD is shown on Figure 6 This chart also shows a surprising factor where it's projected that all the population increases between the present and 2050 AD will occur in the less developed countries:

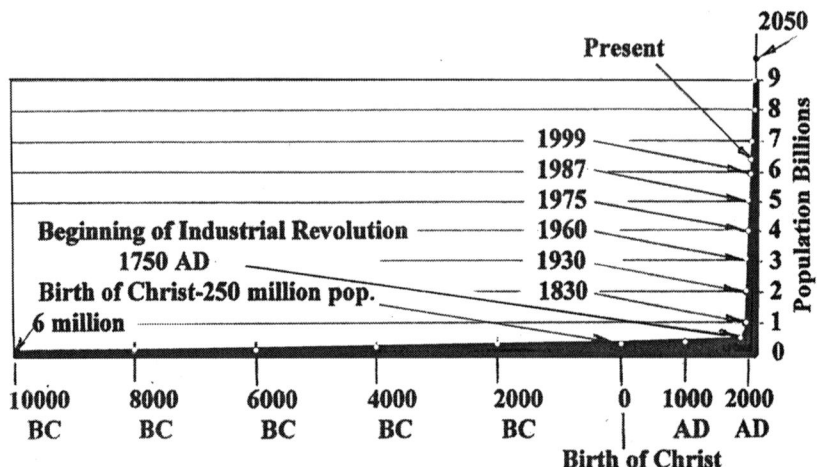

Figure 5 : World Population 1000 BC-Present

Population increases depend on two factors: **increases in the birth rate** and **decreases of the death rate.** Surprisingly small differences in either can quickly change the total population picture. The huge escalation of population growth started soon after the start of the industrial revolution which, among many other things, generated improved health care. This, in turn, helped to lower infant mortality and extends old age which were the principle factors in the radical change in the population curve.

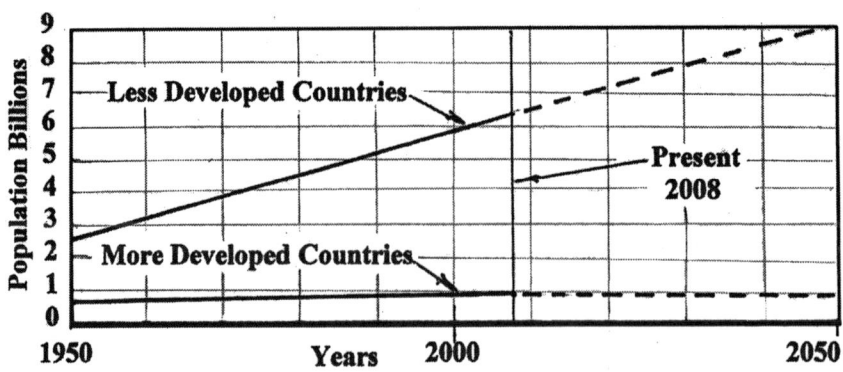

Figure 6: World Total Population 1950-2050

It could be said that we're heading for a Malthusian crisis. This was named after Doctor Thomas Malthus, an English professor who wrote a paper in 1798 on the principles of population. *It stated: Population has a natural tendency to increase faster than the means of subsistence and efforts should be made to cut the birth rate, either by self restraint or birth control.* This in turn brings up the question of what level of population can the planet accommodate? It obviously becomes a critical issue with the total population heading towards 9 billion by 2050 and increasing at the projected rate of 1 billion every twelve years.

Assuming that there will be enough air and water generated by natural cycles, the next essential is food. This will have to be derived by expanding the existing system of farming direct or indirect renewable recyclable crops. It can also be assumed that newcomers to this world will have the desire to eventually rise towards the standard of living levels of the more developed regions. For this to happen, it will be necessary to extend or find renewable replacements for the already hard pressed supply of fossil or other non-renewable resources that are used today for industrial output and construction. It will also be necessary to do this without creating undue waste, pollution and further degradation to the earth's surface.

Even a brief review reveals that resources of fossil and other non-renewables have a finite and limited supply base, and also that the present food system is totally dependent on oil energy for its mass farming and product distribution, and now that the oil age is coming to an end and a renewable based replacement hasn't as yet been determined, it will likely have to revert back to a mixed farming system- farms producing a full range of products. Dealing with waste and pollution issues is also an unresolved problem and even considering a sufficient supply of air and water is most probably a rash assumption. So, it is obvious that any "business as usual" approach will lead to catastrophe, and the brutal hand of nature, or other tragic factors, will take over to control the population to sustainable levels.

The chaotic situation existing in the Middle East is undoubtedly largely caused by the diminishing supply of oil. Further shortages of essential natural elements, i.e. air and water and all non-renewable based minerals materials for industrial use, could provoke further conflicts, including wars, unless some new methods of world management are developed and enforced.

If one is realistic, the only real solution is to follow Dr. Malthus's advice and try to not to let the population explosion progress further until a sustainability program is established. Therefore, the subject of lower fertility rates becomes an all-important question.

The more developed countries are projected to remain at about present population levels in the period up to 2050A.D. All the anticipated population increases are likely to occur in the lesser developed areas of the world such as Asia and Africa. This is particularly true of many of the African countries where life expectancy is low, many of the women are illiterate and purchasing power is minimal. Many of these same countries have male dominant cultures where the woman bear and look after the children, fetch water, run the home, tend animals and grow food. The women have little access to family planning and are often subjected to physical violence and abandonment. Very often, the main occupations of their husbands are drinking, gambling and bragging about their virility and dominance. They often refuse to use contraceptives and are proud of their large families. Living accommodations are sparse, and there is little provision for entertainment, so sexual activity is inevitable, and abortion is usually the women's only means of birth control.

Some countries have instigated successful education programs encouraging women into full family planning decision-making and educating them about available birth controls and to be a participant in the decision-making to have children. Some governments have also developed economic incentives to help control population growth.

These programs and actions are obviously good and in the right direction, but the real solution is to provide occupational activity, work or employment for the males. A great candidate for this comes from the need for returning to an agricultural economy to produce renewable replacements for the diminishing non-renewable materials and the increased need for food.

It is ironic that the Catholic Church is prevalent in many of these developing areas and, unfortunately, is exacerbating the population explosion issue. Their preaching of birth control by abstinence is totally impractical and against Mother Nature, and their attitude against condom usage is hindering not only controlling the fertility rate but also the fight against the spread of sexually transmitted diseases.

There are a whole range of natural disasters which may also reduce the population from time to time. These include: Tsunamis, earthquakes, storms and other violent weather conditions. But the historic numbers of deaths they cause, although tragically large, are comparatively small compared to the population growth in question.

War and conflicts can also decrease the population, but again, the numbers involved are relatively small. In fact, the only meaningful population reducers are provided by nature in the form of famine and disease. However, the world will be in a sorry state if the situation is left to deteriorate for these solutions to become fully into play.

A review of population groups by regions of the world dramatically indicates that the principal concentration is in the Asian and African areas. It is in these same areas that the predominant population growth is anticipated to take place in the first half of the twenty-first century.

Studying lists of statistics on death, birth, literacy and purchasing power brings up a number of important issues including:

- A Zero growth rate equates to approximately a 2.1 fertility which is represented by America's present level.
- That by education programs, financial incentives, use of contraceptives, etc. a number of countries have reduced their fertility rates to less than 2.1 and are now losing population.
- In general, the higher the female literacy rate, the lower the fertility rate and the higher life expectancy and purchasing power.
- Of particular note is the situation in Iran where over the last 10 years an aggressive education program by the Islamic government has produced a large increase in female literacy from 43% to 66%, and a reduction in the fertility rate from 6.6% to 2.3%, together with an increase in purchasing power from $4670 to $5,940 per year.

In the less developed countries, there is obviously a great need to educate the women and put the men to work in order to help control the world's population and to improve living standards.

In the more developed countries where the birth rate is dropping below the 2.1 rate, the break even point, the modern way of life has completely changed many women's point of view on marriage and raising a family. The old approach used to be: first to get married and in one or to two years start having children, attend to the children's upbringing through their school years and into college and run the home and provide room for the children until they were through college and left home, usually to get married and start a similar family cycle of events of their own. Divorce was a rarity and it was expected, or hoped, that the children would be involved with their parent's lives in old age.

Today, many women in the developed world prefer the excitement and interest of working instead of the more mundane life of running the house and bringing up children. Very often they leave home to gain independence and leave marriage until a later date. Many don't marry for sex which, in the liberalized world, is readily available socially. They prefer to continue working rather than be restricted by having children, and they give a variety of reasons for their actions including:

- They don't want to bring children into a world of crime and terrorism.
- They want to preserve their personal freedom without the encumbrance of children.
- They don't want the financial burden of bringing up children reducing their level of disposable income and deterring them from many attractive involvements like world travel, sports and many other varied activities.
- They don't look at the family circle as being an important security in old age.
- They just prefer working as a way of life.
- There are also extreme feminist groups who don't even believe husbands are necessary as sex can be had anytime, anywhere. Also, they can choose same sex marriage and, if desired, acquire test tube babies.

What is puzzling is to hear these same people objecting to immigrants and other less cultured people's taking over the world when they themselves are not willing to keep their country's birth rate above the break even point. They don't seem to realize that when one digs a hole in the beach, it fills with water.

As mentioned previously, disease is one of the factors that influence the population issue. However, up until now, the numbers involved were relatively small. Even the tragic situation with AIDS and its spread internationally is still not enough to be meaningful in affecting world population. But there is a new disease that quietly arrived on the scene and is growing at an alarming rate. It goes under the name of **Obesity,** and its full impact has yet to be determined, together with its cause and effect; obviously, it can be partially attributed to a whole range of issues including:

- Eating too much
- Eating and drinking unsuitable foods and liquids.
- Not exercising sufficiently.

Each of these factors obviously plays a large part in the total obesity equation, but it does not explain why there has been such a large increase in a period of 20 years or so. To observe obesity it is necessary only to go to a shopping mall and watch the world go by. Observers would be alarmed at the number of obese humans in the Western World. Many of these individuals are alarmingly fat to a level where they find it difficult to walk and are obviously impeded in performing the normal functions of running a home or performing physical duties in the workplace. It still doesn't explain the suddenness of the increase nor explain why it occurs? It is difficult to generalize, but by observation a high proportion of obese persons are from poorer classes.

The effects of obesity are many and varied and, at this stage, largely undefined. As already mentioned, it limits a person's ability to participate in physical activity. It sometimes prevents them from participating in social occasions and causes a variety of medical problems, i.e. Heart disease, diabetes, worn-out joints and limbs, high blood pressure and difficulty in traveling. Even general living presents problems such as just fitting into chairs, beds, cars and general transportation vehicles. Some airlines have already reacted by charging for the extra space. Obtaining clothes becomes a serious issue, and low self-esteem is one of the many psychological problems that go with it. It is seemingly not transmissible but one sees whole families with the problem. This is obviously explainable by them all participating in the same eating habits. Life expectancy is clearly lower than that of normal persons and brings up the question "Could it seriously affect the nation's ability to exist and progress?" It is hard to say at this stage, but it needs further study in case it becomes a possibility.

One of the issues that are known to affect obesity is the advent of fast food restaurants with their highly sugared, fattening foods and drinks together with their ready availability. There is also the open issue of general food nutrient content and any genetic link, which is more difficult to define. Mass-produced foods, selling in fast food restaurants and supermarkets, are produced with mass farming techniques and all have basically become established in the last 50 years, and their effects have not as yet been fully defined and rationalized.

When growing products and raising cattle changed from mixed farming, using natural bio-based procedures, to mass farming using chemicals for feed, fertilizer and soil preparation, food nutrient content went through a radical change. The natural recycling of land use changed to a preparation of soil using chemicals which kill most of the basic creatures in the lower food chain such as worms, beetles and insects and leaves a chemical residue which can migrate into the produce. Whatever effect this has on the human body systems is not generally known and may be one of the principle factors causing obesity. As one researcher found, rice grown in Bangladesh, China and Latin America is some 15-25% more nutritious than irrigated rice grown in the

United States. Hopefully, the anticipated change back from mass farming to mixed farming will be accompanied by a change back to bio-based preparation products. Only time will tell, but in the meantime, the obesity disease is running rampant and affecting many of the more developed countries. One has only to watch TV news and look at current school class group photographs to become totally alarmed at the young age at which obesity can be seen. It brings up the obvious fact that just looking at population statistics can be misleading. The mental and physical aspects of the people affected by obesity are also extremely important if we are to succeed in achieving the objectives of sustainability.

The change from mixed to mass farming was caused by the demand for more food and obviously to be more profitable. The change also required more machinery and transportation equipment and, consequently, more gasoline. The oil crisis and a renewable replacement for oil will be the main influencing factors causing us to refocus on mixed farming.

It doesn't look as though man-made wars or natural disasters will have any real meaningful effect on the population growth issue. However, diseases like AIDS and **Obesity** could have serious consequences depending on how mankind handles the problem. It may turn out that saving the beetles and worms at the base of the food chain might, in turn, help save the human race from destroying itself. But the priority issue for solving the population problem still has to be providing agricultural occupational opportunity for the males in the less developed countries; this in turn will bring education and a meaningful reduction in the birthrate.

As stated, population change is the difference between the birth rate and the death rate. As it's not "socially correct" to tamper with increasing the death rate, efforts will have to be concentrated on decreasing the birthrate in order to reach a sustainability level. The emerging battle for the usage of recyclable crops as a means of re-placing non-renewables, however, could easily erupt into a mass world shortage of food, and a high level of death and disease would not be far behind. This would mean that nature would be largely responsible for solving the population problem in a very ugly way.

Chapter 5
ENERGY

Energy is the capacity to do work, and it comes in many forms starting with the combination of ingredients that feeds the vegetation in the natural cycle of events. This, in turn, provides the basis for the start of the food chain that generates the food for all living creatures. This same base, combined with Mother Nature's continuous ongoing recyclable forms of renewable power including air, water, solar, hydro, wind, geothermal, etc., provides much of the energy to support man's need to maintain the "Wondrous World" we live in today. All of this energy comes, or came, either directly or indirectly from the sun. Creating this energy can range from the sun's rays nourishing a tiny biological cell to all that is embedded in the non-renewable materials enacted by the sun during the earth's formation period when large quantities of materials were absorbed into the still molten mass.

We have to be reminded that every article or action in this wondrous world is comprised of a spectrum of energy factors which becomes part of its **Embedded Energy Equation (EEE)**.

This starts with the range of energies that are involved with the growing or mining and processing of the basic materials involved together with manufacturing and multiple transportation factors that all become part of the embedded energy equation.

A simple subject like a stainless steel spoon has a complex energy equation. The stainless steel contains iron, nickel, carbon and minor amounts of other elements. All of these have to be separately extracted from the earth by energy driven mining equipment and processed and transported by energy burning machines to a point where they can be blended together by energy burning furnaces to make stainless steel. The steel ingots are converted into stainless steel sheets and transported to a spoon manufacturer who stamps or forges them into spoon forms and then processes them through cropping and polishing to a finished product which is packed for shipping: All these phases involve expenditures of energy. The boxes of spoons are subsequently shipped to a dealer's warehouse and held until an order is received from a retailer. Getting the spoons to the outlet takes several more energy burning transport operations until eventually they arrive at a shop. The shop displays the spoons, which requires physical labor, and then they are eventually sold to a customer who takes them home and puts them in a cutlery drawer. Equating the multitude of contents and actions for the spoons EEE is done by using the inbuilt dollar value of each stage which all ends up as part of their selling price.

One also has to remember that all non-renewables will eventually have to be replaced with renewable materials even if they are not due to become exhausted for hundreds of years or more. In the simple case of a spoon there are a whole range of renewable-based plastics that can be, and are now being, used in making spoons. The real problem comes with more complicated items such as automobiles which are made up of several hundred dif-

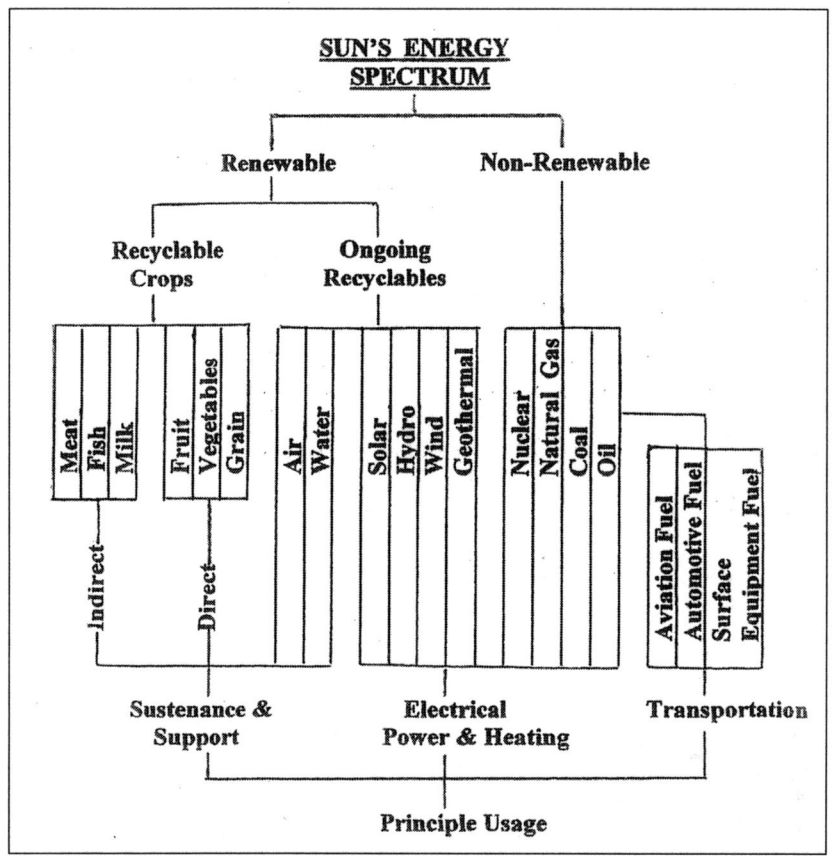

Figure 7: The Sun's Energy Spectrum.

ferent components with varying ingredients, each with their own embedded energy equation. This involves a monumental listing with a multitude of non-renewable items which will eventually have to be substituted by renewables. At this stage this sounds an impossible task, but good long-term planning will help to find the required answers. Firstly, one thinks of how to replace the engine block and pistons which are subject to extreme heat. Well, in the period we are dealing with, the internal combustion engine will have been replaced with electric fuel cells where the energy is generated by chemical interaction and not explosive heat from burning the fuel. This opens up a multitude of material substitution possibilities. Specialty cars have already been built using adhesives instead of nuts and bolts for assembly, and cars are already being built using plastics in place of metals for the basic body and chassis structures. It all illustrates the need and the importance of long-term planning and standing far enough back in time for reviewing what seems, at first blush, to be impossible.

The sun's energy spectrum can be categorized as shown in Figure 7 which shows the group split into the renewable and non-renewable types. The chart then tracks them to their principal utilization of **Nutritional-Sustenance -- Electrical Power and Heating -- Transportation.**

Nutritional- Sustenance: At the inception of life on earth there was a parallel action of generating plant life. This vegetation became the basic sustenance for feeding all living creatures and evolved from recyclable crops which were nurtured by the sun's rays and the earth's movements which cause day and night and the seasons of the year. The other essentials to maintain life are air (oxygen) and water which are ongoing renewable cycles provided by the sun.

This cycle of events has continued until today, estimated to be over 3 billion years later, when over 6 billion humans and all other living creatures are still nourished by the suns renewable blessings. This is done either directly by the consumption of fruit and vegetables or indirectly by meat, fish and fowl who in turn exist by feeding on the sun's products.

The nutrition provided by the sun in the form of food is, by definition, the most important category of energy as it is the basic supporter of life. Once again one is reminded that every living creature has to have its daily supply of food, and it is amazing that this has been maintained despite the huge growth in human population. It also re-emphasizes that nature selected this form of energy supply derived from renewable recyclable crops as opposed to using one time available fossil based materials. This process has been labeled as **Nature's Way** and is the direction we have to progressively turn to for the rest of our needs

Electricity -This second category of energy is used to produce and maintain the products we use in our daily lives. These include the houses we live in, our cars and all the manufactured items we use that allow us to live a life of comfort and convenience. This energy comes to us mainly in the form of **Electricity** which powers many of our appliances and provides heat and light. It also provides the power for all our communication units, including computers, together with reproducing machines and a full spectrum of office equipment and gadgets. The form of electricity we use is a clean and efficient product that is easy to handle. It can be produced by natural processes such as hydro, wind and solar, but the largest share at present is produced by burning dirty fossil fuels including coal, oil and natural gas which all produce large quantities of undesirable pollutants that are released into the atmosphere. Coal, the dirtiest burning, is also produced by mining which has the associated negative of surface degradation. Another source of electricity is nuclear power which, although having a cleaner production process, does also have a very serious issue of disposing of its atomic waste byproducts. The uranium used in this fission process is another non-renewable based material having a finite supply base which is mined and, again, causes extensive surface degradation. There is some research into using the fusion process, as used by the sun, but this has unbelievably high temperature, handling and control problems.

There are, however, some other more practical possibilities of which geothermal is the most promising. The center of the earth is a hot mass and can be tapped by deep drilling, and the heat can easily be converted into electricity which could become a major source of supply by providing a non-polluting abundance of power. There is some use of this process today, and larger installations are being researched.

In the more developed countries we use electricity at every twist and turn of our busy lives. Flicking a switch is almost second nature in order for people to generate a desired response, ranging from lighting to heating and a myriad of other services. Electricity is also used extensively in factories and places of business to minimize manual labor. Electricity is, in itself, a clean, convenient power supply which can be generated from many sources as shown in Figure 8. These range from ongoing recyclables to all the principal fossil based materials.

The following chart shows a rough breakdown of these electricity generating sources in comparison to the total world wide energy picture. These estimates are based on the year 2000 and do not include nutritional (Food) energy factors.

As the Figure shows, low polluting renewables, at this stage, account for only about 20% of the electricity generating base, while high pollutants account for 80% with coal being the largest single item at 40%. Replacing coal, natural gas and oil with low polluting renewables for generating electricity is obviously a formidable task.

Despite its many virtues, electricity does have some problems, of which storage is the major issue. Batteries are the principal method of storing electricity but do have a limitation with respect to capacity. They are fine for powering watches and flashlights and are a means of storing electricity on automobiles for starting the engine, lighting and running all the accessories. They are even practical as a principal power source on electric vehicles such as golf carts, vans and cars. They are also used extensively in portable

World Energy Base%			World Electricity Base%		
Coal	24	High	Coal	40	High
Nat. Gas	21	Pollutants	Nat. Gas.	16	Pollutants
Oil	35	High	Oil	8	80%
Nuclear*	6	86%	Nuclear*	16	
Hydro	3	Low	Hydro	18	Low
Other#	>1	Pollutants	Other#	2	Pollutants
Solid Biomass	10	14%			20%
Total Content Energy Base	100%		100%= 13% of World Energy Base		

Notes: * Nuclear has an unsolved waste problem.
 # Other includes Renewables: Wind, Solar, Wave Action, Waste, Biomass, Geothermal, etc.
 -Solid Biomass is mainly Wood.

Figure 8: The World's Energy Base vs. Generated Electricity Base

equipment i.e. tools, vacuums, laptops, etc. but quickly become impractical for high voltage power usage such as the general electrical supply.

The storage issue is the principle problem with electricity and necessitates that it be used as it's made and requires a distribution grid. The grid tries to balance usage variation between customers, but this complicated action is limited by distance. It does not, at present, have the capability to cover the total variation of usage between day and night which can only be achieved by a worldwide grid. This will involve transporting the power over great distances with associated efficiency losses. But at some point in the future, it may be possible with superconductors or the invention of wireless transmission of electricity. As and when this happens, unification of voltages and frequencies would be of great advantage, and the whole system would need international involvement. Keeping generators running at a constant rate would also go a long way to helping the lack of storage capability. Meanwhile, high efficiency battery development is continuing for smaller sized power applications.

The academic world has proposed linking hydrogen production by electrolyses as a means of storing electricity. The hydrogen would be stored in massive high pressure containers when produced and then converted back into electricity by running generators when needed. Unfortunately, the conversion losses would absorb an impractical amount of the power involved, so it is not likely that this, or any other double conversion method, will be used for storing electricity.

If conversion to renewable clean materials and processes is not forthcoming soon enough to meet the pollution requirements, an electricity conservation program may also be necessary. This is likely to be some decades into the future but because we have been so nonchalant with electricity usage it should be not be difficult to make considerable savings relatively easily.

As stated, geothermal is the principal potential new source for generating electricity. Deep boring techniques are being developed' and the heat energy locked below the earth's crust is sitting there waiting to be used. The heat at the center of the earth, because of its immense size, makes it virtually a bottomless pit. The conversion of heat to electricity is a straightforward established process and is accomplished with negligible pollution and very little ground degradation. Developments with wind, sun, wave action, etc. and other possible ongoing recyclables are also continuing, and all these should eventually contribute to the displacement of coal and other dirty fuels used today and help in leading us to a more sustainable future.

Transportation- The third and special category of energy is used for transportation which is almost totally based on **Oil**. This is a most critical segment as much of the world's needs for living involve a multiplicity of transportation factors. These range from the shipment of all materials during and between production operations to the delivery to the final user with all land, sea and air transportation, including personal passenger vehicles. It is also fundamental to the farming, processing and delivery of all food products.

Oil is also the first of the high usage, vital non-renewable based materials to approach the situation where in the near future supply will not meet demand. Therefore, costs will continue to escalate.

Figure 9 is fundamentally interesting because it is the estimate of how much oil each area of the world started with and also estimates how much still remains. These figures are based on the USGS (United States Geographical Survey) as published in the CRS report for Congress:

It will be noted that the United States' original endowment, as distributed by Mother Nature in the creation of the world, was 260 billion barrels of oil. (One barrel = 42 gallons) As can be seen, this number was the second-largest in the world, tied with Russia and only exceeded by Saudi Arabia. Saudi Arabia still has 80% of its endowment, and Russia has 64%. But unlike these other countries, the United States has only 35% left. The question may well be asked "How come?" This can be explained very simply by the fact that America used more oil more quickly. The USA was essentially the discoverer of oil and immediately started using it in the mid-19th century for lighting purposes. This was followed by the invention of the internal combustion engine and automobiles toward the end of the century. Then, most importantly, Americans began the mass production of automobiles in the first 20 years of the 20th century. This period also included WWI (1914 – 1918),

Country	Original Oil Endowment	Remaining Oil
Saudi Arabia*	377	302
Russia	262	168
United States	260	92
Iran*	152	108
Iraq*	149	126
Venezuela*	130	82
Kuwait*	128	100
UAE*	118	102
Mexico	96	74
China	87	67
Libya*	56	37
Canada	49	33
Kazakhstan	47	43
Nigeria*	41	25
United Kingdom	38	25
Indonesia*	34	19
Norway	31	23
Brazil	27	23
Algeria*	19	9
Malaysia	14	11
Egypt	14	7
Azerbaijan	14	7
Colombia	13	9
Oman*	13	9
Turkmenistan	13	8
India	12	8
Argentina	12	6
Qatar*	11	6
Australia	10	6
Angola	9	6
Ecuador	7	5
Romania	7	3
Tunisia	7	3
Yemen*	6	6
Uzbekistan	5	5
Brunei	5	2
Trinidad	5	2

* OPEC member

Figure 9: Comparison of original oil endowment and estimated remaining reserves by country shown in billions of barrels.

where land vehicles using oil were employed; however, this coincided with the fighting Navy's of the USA and England converting to oil usage rather than coal. Also, the USA, in its generosity, became the supplier of much of the oil for World War I.

The accelerated development of this Wondrous World largely took place in America between WW I and WW II when transportation greatly expanded, particularly in the automotive segment. In other words, America "got there first" and consequently used its oil reserves more quickly. Again in World War II America became a substantial oil supplier to the Allied armies. After WWII the U.S. also embarked on a fast road to establishing the highest standard of living in the world which was largely based on transportation factors. All this came at a heavy cost in oil usage culminating today in only 35% of US oil remaining.

This all led to the situation that exists today where the USA is by far the biggest user of oil in the world using roughly 25% of the world's oil production of 94 million barrels per day. This includes all liquid fuels, i.e., propane, LNG, etc.

This situation has already developed into world crises which will not be fully rectified until a renewable replacement for oil is established and in effect. Figure 10 shows the progressively increasing degree of the oil shortfall. This is particularly disturbing when one realizes that an oil replacement has not yet been agreed upon and certainly not practically proven. Even when the decision is made on an acceptable material, it will take a number of years for development and to build up the production volume to balance the oil deficiency. These timing issues are shown in Figure 10 and the explanatory notes included therewith:

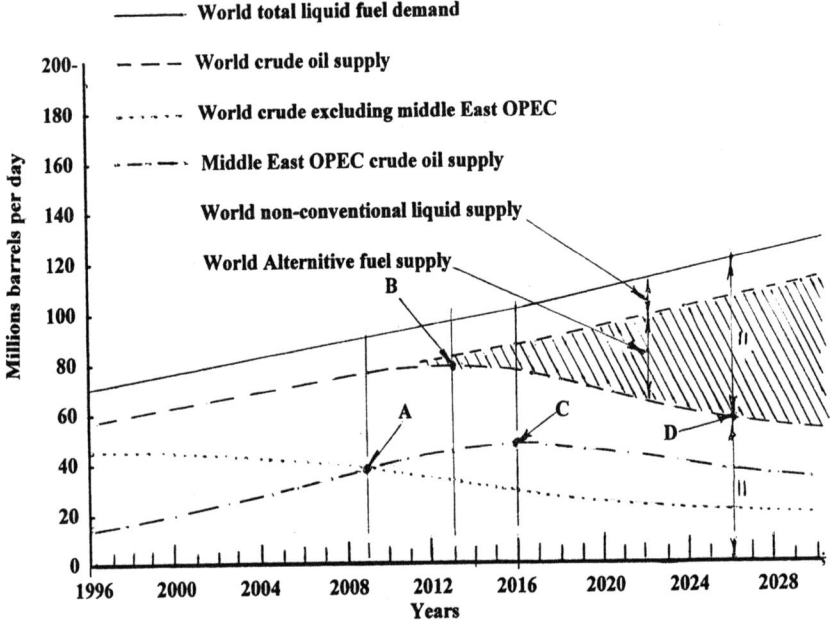

Figure 10: World demand for liquid fuel balanced against supply

Summary of oil supply milestones- Millions of barrels per day

Date-year	Point A 2009	Point B 2013	Point C 2016	Point D 2026
Total demand for liquid fuels	94	99	103	122
Total propane & other non-conventional liquids	14	14	14	14
Total alternative fuel	-	3	9	47
Middle East OPEC crude	40	48	49	39
World crude excluding Middle East OPEC	40	34	31	22
World total liquid fuel supply	94	99	103	122

Point A is the year 2009 when Mid. East OPEC equals the rest of the world supply.

Point B is the year 2013 when the world's oil supply is predicted to peak out.

Point C is the year 2016 when Mid. East OPEC is predicted to peak out.

Point D is the year 2026 when the world's supply of alternative fuels plus non-conventional liquids must equal oil

These numbers are based on realistic reserves of recoverable oil being 2,300 billion barrels. Other, more optimistic, numbers assume 3,000 billion barrels, but these include oil sand, heavy oil and other materials which may not be practical to recover.

At present, the total world supply and demand of liquid fuel is balanced at about 94 million barrels per day. The U.S. normally uses about 24 million barrels of this for its domestic consumption, of which approximately 14 million is used in the transportation sector (About 9 million for surface equipment and cars, 3 million for trucks and 2 million for aircraft). About 70% of the 24 million barrels are imported.

Many people mislead themselves by calculating the anticipated average daily usage of oil, possibly, 120 million barrels per day over the next 40 years. With the available recoverable oil reserves being approximately 2,300 billion barrels and extrapolating how long it will last into the future, the supply should last about 50 years. They, therefore, assume that we have plenty of fuel left, and there is no immediate panic. The fact they miss is that the point in time when we grovel in the sand for the last gallon is not important. The critical point is reached when supply does not meet demand, and this occurs as one will see on the chart, in about 2013, at point B. Also, as this point is approached, the supply of oil becomes tenuous, and any happening such as a Mid-Eastern crisis or a broken pipeline will be reflected in immediate price increases. The international oil situation is further aggravated by the fact that America has less than 5% of the world's population but uses 25 % of the world's oil, of which 70% is imported.

The government has not responded to the situation by either a meaningful conservation program or by emphasizing and supporting the critical need for developing a renewable replacement for oil.

It All Started With 9/11

Meanwhile, large, gas guzzling vehicles have become the norm, but even with the escalated oil price, as high as $4, Americans are still only paying about one half the price Europeans pay ($8). This is largely because the European governments heavily tax fuel to give them a source of revenues and, more importantly, to encourage smaller and more efficient vehicles. This is something that the American government could also do, but the logic to accept such a proposal will be very difficult to present to politicians or the public.

Figure 11 shows the top 10 oil uses together with other relevant to data. As will be seen, the United States' usage of **20,655** million barrels per day is outrageously high compared to other countries. It is also different from the previous levels of 24 million barrels quoted in this book because it does not include non-conventional liquid fuels, i.e. propane.

Country	Land Size 000sq km	Population mil	Economy GDP $ bn	Defense Spending $ bn	Armed Forces Reg+Res 000	Ownership cars per 000 pop	Crude Oil usage mil bar/day
United States	9,373	298	12,417	495	2,479	465	^ 20,655
China	9,561	1,316	2,234	104	3,055	10	6,988
Japan	378	128	4,534	44	283	441	5,360
Russia	17,075	143	764	66*	21,027	157*	2,753
Germany	358	83	2,795	38	246*	546	2,586
India	3,287	1,103	806	22	2,471	8	2,485
South Korea	99	48	787	20	5,187	218	2,308
Canada	9,971	32	1,114	13	63*	561	2,241
Mexico	1,973	107	768	6*	278	142	1,978
France	544	60	2,127	53	277	495	1,961

Notes: Most of the above data was extracted from the Economist 2008 Pocket World in Figures and are mostly 2004-7 vintage. Figures marked with * are from other sources and are dated 2007. All numbers are prior to the affect of the recession.
^ Excludes unconventional fuel liquids, i.e. LPG and propane.

Figure 11: The top 10 countries by crude oil fuel usage.

Chapter 6

ENVIRONMENT

When life on this planet started evolving some 3-4 billion years ago, the ingredients selected by Mother Nature generated a totally sustainable existence. This was achieved by using sun-based renewable materials provided by the land, sea and air coupled with byproducts from their usage being totally recycled back into nature's systems. For example, excreta (urine and feces) were totally returned to the ground's surface to become part of the soil's regenerative cycle. This condition continued until a few hundred years ago when man chose to start exploiting fossils and other non-renewable materials as a means of improving his comfort and convenience. These materials initially included iron and coal together with other materials and elements which had detrimental byproducts of their usage which could not be returned to nature's natural cycles. This started the degradation of the earth's surface by destructive actions such as mining, clearing forests, dumping garbage and waste into streams, rivers and oceans and releasing the pollution from burning wood and coal into the atmosphere. Fortunately, at this time the population was less than 1 billion, and the devastation was containable.

By present day standards life was relatively simple but harsh, and humans, with their inbuilt desire to improve their circumstances, started to invent new products and devices to reduce physical work and improve the comfort and convenience of their existence. To do this, they made use of every readily available commodity and material that came to hand regardless of its impact on the earth and its effect on future generations. This haphazard activity proceeded without any ongoing long-term planning, and, therefore, the industrial age commenced during the 18th century with all its ugly pollution and degradation without appropriate controls. With an insatiable need and desire for wood, they indiscriminately stripped forests for use both as a fuel and construction material, and they started to mine the earth's surface for every conceivable material and chemical which left a trail of surface degradation.

The resulting industrial action was also starting to spew pollution into the atmosphere on the assumption that the mighty universe could absorb it. As a means of improving and revolutionizing transportation, various machines were invented for land and sea travel, and man continued to colonize and build empires on a world wide basis. It was an ugly time when uncontrolled development activities gave birth to whole industrial towns with the associated populations shift from the country to the city. It was a time when factories burned raw coal for power, and nearly every home used it for heating and cooking. This resulted in blackened towns with an industrial haze hanging in the air. Any inversion condition in the air was likely to bring the sulphur laden clouds down to ground level which caused an unbelievably thick fog. In London, England this set of conditions created the infamous "pea soup fog" where it was not possible to see an outstretched hand in front of one's face.

Basically, all factories use large amounts of water. Originally, this water was dumped into waterways after being used without any processing. Waste and sewage collection and disposal was accomplished by primitive systems which also added to the environmental degradation. Waste and garbage was dumped in open pits, and sewage residue was emptied into rivers, streams and oceans where it was hoped that the food chain and time would look after its dissipation.

As time proceeded into the mid 1800's, oil was discovered, and, although initially refined for use in lamp lighting applications, it soon became the fuel of choice for the newly invented internal combustion engines (ICE's). These engines became the motivational power for all forms of vehicles that started their long domination of the all important transportation industry. Although oil is a cleaner burning material than coal, it is still very dirty. When oil is converted to gasoline for automotive fuel, it generates large quantities of pollutants; refining and transporting the fuel adds still more.

While all this activity was proceeding, the population was escalating at an incredible rate. Since 1830 when the first billion was reached, it has increased to 6.4 billion in 2007 and is projected to rise to 9 billion by 2050. This factor has exacerbated and accentuated all the problems involved, and today the pattern of using coal and oil for generating power and fuel has continued. Although controls have helped clean up exhausts, huge amounts of carbon dioxide and other gases and particulates are still being belched into the atmosphere. Scientific proof has finally convinced the world politicians that the affect on the atmosphere is causing non-reversible detrimental conditions, such as global warming.

Although this subject has produced some discussion, there is still only limited meaningful corrective reaction at this stage.

These issues have no boundaries, and whoever in the world creates a problem shares it with all. When discussing new systems or processes, you hear diabolical statements like, "We will locate the new plant to produce this material in the middle of the desert. Or, "We will sequester the contaminated byproducts by burying them in the ground." This attitude is ridiculously short sighted and totally ignores the future. Such people refuse to acknowledge that the atmosphere and oceans are internationally connected, and any individual action affecting them becomes a global issue.

Most of the elements and basic materials were scientifically known and their usage defined by 1800 AD and many of these non-renewable substances had become the subject of mining quests. This aggressive mining commenced on the premise of immediate need, although everybody knew that all these materials had a finite "only created once" lifespan. But they seemingly did not care or give consideration to these materials ever becoming extinct. Even today, the more commonly used materials such as oil, iron, cement and brass etc. are viewed as if their supply will basically go on to eternity. Again, the problem of people refusing to plan beyond their lifespan is the major deterrent to rational long term planning. The factual premise that all fossil and non-renewable based materials have a limited supply base has not influenced the thought processes of most people. Many of these common materials are now entering the first phase of the extinction process. Demand is excessively escalating the price beyond the normal economic growth values. The obvious reason is the more developed countries have established the materials usage in advancing their standard of living, and now the developing countries are emulating them with construction, manufacturing and transportation industries aiming at the standard of living set by the West. All this is exacerbated by the evolution of communication tools, i.e. the World Wide Web. China and India are prime examples of developing countries that are now the major users of many such materials like iron and cement.

All non-renewables will eventually need replacement by renewable materials, and it is self-evident that many of these replacements will have to be derived from recyclable crops or ongoing natural resources such as sun, wind, hydro, wave action, geothermal, etc. Until these replacements are available, a conservation program is vital to extend the availability of the old material resources as long as possible and hopefully still control further damage to the earth's surface. This last comment refers to the fact that all the non-renewable materials have to be mined to extract them from the earth, and this mining process has already destroyed large areas of the earth's surface. If left to their own devices, the coal mining operations will go on supplying coal despite the land destruction and even though it is one of the most atmospheric contaminating materials and is a major contributor to global warming. They will go on mining to make a dollar even if it leaves the earth's surface looking like the moon.

It is highly likely that the replacement for most non-renewables, will be derived from recyclable crops such as trees and other vegetation. This again emphasizes the need to protect remaining farm and arable land by minimizing mining with its devastating affects.

Oil is one of the first critical commodities that are now reaching a point where its demand will soon exceed the supply. Because of the importance of oil to the all important transportation sector, the price has already reached the level of starting to destabilize the economies of the world. It has already destabilized the peace of the world by the Middle East conflicts that are ongoing largely because of oil. To find a renewable replacement for oil that has minimal pollution factors in its production and usage is one of the world's most urgent problems to solve. This is not only to help minimize pollution, but to keep the world functioning.

The subject of sewage disposal of human and commercial waste is another vitally important subject that has wandered off course. It is also an issue which relates very closely to the ever-increasing importance of water supply and quality.

Until a few hundred years ago, humans deposited their excreta randomly on the soil surface. The top layer of soil absorbed the remaining nutrients to once more become part of its recycling ecosystem. This largely kept any contaminates out of the underlying surface water drainage system. At that time Asian farmers recognized the value of human and animal excreta for its nutrient value in recharging the soil and they continued to plow the excreta back into the land's surface. Whereas, the Western World took an attitude that excreta is something unpleasant and should be disposed of. These philosophies have continued until the present day where Asian countries utilize their human waste as fertilizer, and the Western world has continued to mix it into their general waste system which results in an unusable and difficult to dispose of toxic sludge.

When water was piped directly into homes in the early 19th century, the Western world coupled it into the waste system to help send the sewage though the pipes. This not only used large quantities of drinking water but also washed out the nitrogen from the urine which largely destroys the chemical action between the urine and the feces nullifying it's usage as a fertilizer. Once the sewer system was installed, industry saw the opportunity for a cheap way of dumping most of its general wastes. This combination of excreta and industrial and household wastes has to be processed until it becomes a pile of toxic sludge with much of the nutrients washed out; then it has to be disposed of. This has been found to be very difficult because when dumped into oceans or other bodies of water it creates large polluted dead zones. This practice was outlawed by governmental rule in 1992. Now utilities are trying to find other methods such as burning or burying to dispose of the sludge, but the whole system needs revamping in keeping with *sustainability requirements.* That is, the system's actions must reuse and recycle all byproducts without leaving any non-usable residue.

It requires the separate handling of the excreta with a dry collection system such as used in aircraft and boats with most probably individual home collection units as used in some Eastern countries. This will provide the opportunity for human waste to become a separate collectable like other waste products to be taken to a central specialized processing center. It will also require commercial industrial establishments to stop dumping their waste in the public system and develop their own methods of disposing and handling of their own special wastes. This, of course, will become a much easier problem when manufacturing switches to renewable based materials for achieving sustainability. The other biodegradables from household waste can still be disposed of through the existing garbage disposal and drain system and separated later in the processing plant to become biomass which can then be used in many ways for generating energy products.

These actions will save vast amounts of valuable water and get away from dumping our sewage in our drinking water sources. Revising the system will take a long term planning program, many dollars and much time; way beyond a single lifespan. The action is unavoidable and will have to be accomplished at some point to achieve sustainability. It is surprising that such a critical issue has, over centuries, been allowed to become a political football and highly influenced by industry with its short term planning based on the almighty dollar preventing a fundamental resolution.

The change from an agricultural to an industrial economy

in the nineteenth century, coupled with the rapidly expanding population, brought with it some new production supply problems. It was found that the naturally occurring elements and the established cultivation methods were insufficient to provide the increased food yields required. Therefore, it was decided to pursue artificial replacements using chemical based instead of natural materials for their soil preparation ingredients. The materials ranged from animal feed to insecticides, fungicides to fertilizers, etc., and it was found that phosphate could be used as a substitute ingredient in many of these products. Unfortunately, phosphate is produced by strip mining that not only ruins thousands of acres of land and uses huge amounts of valuable water but also results in producing difficult to dispose of poisonous by-products which find their way into the groundwater system. Florida is one of the favored states for such activities with new sites still being approved for mining. This is happening when old, used-up sites are blights on the landscape and contaminate the environment with their overloaded pits of poisonous byproducts. This is a result of conglomerates forming companies and making wonderful promises of "cleaning-up afterwards" in order to receive mining approval. After they have exploited the land, these clean-up promises are seemingly conveniently forgotten. Sometimes the companies even go bankrupt and the owners and shareholders evaporate over the horizon with their profits. In some cases local authorities are left with the expense and difficult job of cleaning up and disposing of the dangerous chemical residues. This is then done at the taxpayers' expense and with great harm to surrounding countryside and waterways. The land involved is virtually useless and is dangerously contaminated.

Mining for coal is another major destroyer of surface lands even when done with the old dangerous underground tunneling process which generates massive amounts of dirt and debris. It is even more disastrous when "open strip mining" is employed. One new approach is to remove the tops of the hills and swells by dynamite blasting to expose the coal seams. The result is, again, even worse degradation; further land use for farming is hard to imagine. Local authorities should think very carefully before giving licenses and ruining land forever in exchange for the one-time dollars to help local budgets.

It is surprising how little media attention is given to the degradation factors created by mining. This is particularly bewildering as material demands are increasing while the easily extractables are diminishing. This requires accepting lower quality materials such as low grade ores, oil shale, etc., and necessitates the use of other more difficult to extract materials. This intense exploitation of mineral rich land is rapidly increasing the degraded areas and diminishing usable land available for agriculture. The amount of mining waste is radically increasing. For instance, in Canada, a heavily mined country, it has been estimated that mining waste is 60 times greater then urban garbage.

A major factor in the pollution equation is not only the by-products of a materials usage, but also the consequences of its production processes. A good example is oil which is a material that has been sitting harmlessly in the ground for millions of years. The trouble starts when the crude oil is brought to the surface. At that point, it has to be shipped to a refinery and becomes vulnerable to mishaps like the Valdez disaster. Once it reaches the refinery, it starts a series of processes which release various toxic pollutants into the atmosphere. The final products are not only gasoline and diesel fuel but a raft of other materials including tar for resurfacing roads. Another series of pollutants are produced when these products are put to use. Oil fuels, whether combusted in engines or used to generate power, produce toxic exhaust gases. The processing of tar into asphalt and applying it as a road surface also generates undesirable gases and particulates. As the products are shipped between each stage, it also generates pollutants from the transportation vehicles. The overall pollution factor is the production+usage+shipping. Returning again to the subject of a conservation program brings up the subject of recycling.

As one starts to look at the long term affects-outside one's life span-, it becomes clear that we can't afford to dispose of anything without using it to its fullest as all materials and elements are forms of embedded energy and will eventually be depleted. Some materials such as metals have a very simple process of meltdown for their recycling. Other materials are more complex with various elements, and it is more difficult to find an efficient method of recycling. The subject of where to dispose of waste is an important issue because we can't afford to dispose of any embedded energy until we have investigated possible further reuse. The importance of this will become more evident as the non-renewables we use become exhausted. We need to aim for a cycle of self support with basically the only new inputs being those the sun can provide (renewables) and with zero waste.

Recycling is an operation that has been going on for many years but was only prevalent with large sized items such as cars and ships. Old discarded cars have been compressed and shipped to foundries where they can be melted down and reprocessed, and ships have always had breaker yards where they can be progressively taken apart and again sent back to foundries for meltdown. It is only more recently that the term "recycling" has started to be used for more mundane items such as bottles, cans, paper, garden rubbish, etc.

It has been realized that undue amounts of plastic and paper have become involved with wrapping and serving products. Having wrapped, bagged or canned the products once for shipping the question of "Paper or plastic?' is still asked at the supermarket for the convenience of carrying the items to the buyer's car. This action has resulted in huge amounts of added debris being taken to the garbage dump. Unfortunately paper uses wood in its manufacturer, and plastic is often derived from petroleum based materials which can sometimes take over a thousand years to degrade in the dump.

Also, many people have become obsessed with drinking liquids, including water, from plastic bottles. These, when discarded, often get recycled, but others find their way to the dump and add to the degrading problem.

The situation is progressively being responded to by countries, towns or other authorities which are requiring the buyers to bring their own carrier bags. This action is solving part of a problem, and designer bags are even being produced to encourage their usage. The drinking bottles, however, are another problem. Some get recycled, but others still become an overload on the garbage system, and all are a drain on the energy system. Some areas have banned their use as water bottles and just say the public water supply from the faucet is good enough. It's going to be interesting to see whether this will be effective and see what other ideas, such as more and better home water purification units to slow the use of plastic bottles and other containers, develop.

The issue of recycling becomes even more complex when it is applied to the subject of buildings which contain huge quantities of embedded energy. These can vary from private homes to massive sky-scraper complexes all of which use cement, steel and wood as primary building materials. The question is what happens when these materials start to approach depletion and renewable replacements have to be found? Different approaches to building will have to be developed. For instance, one can visualize possible new synthetic materials being more suitable for horizontal homebuilding construction instead of vertical skyscrapers. Wood can continue to be used, but it will be in conjunction with the synthetic materials developed from renewables. This action item might be conducive to the changing way of life that may exist at that time. Already, new electronic communication systems have dispensed with much of the need for people to be gathered closely together to run companies and other activities. Also, the limited availability of transportation energy is likely to generate even more work at home type activities.

Another aspect of the building construction will be the longevity factor. Although today large buildings have reasonably lengthy life expectancy, smaller buildings such as homes have life expectancies diminished down in many cases to less than 100 years. Buildings have huge amounts of embedded energy inbuilt, and to dispose of relatively new structures with a wrecking ball only to put another chunk of embedded energy in its place is unduly wasteful. It will encourage more enduring designs that can be adapted to long term usage. Even today, one can see a marked difference between America and Europe. Upper class homes in the U.S. are often scrapped after 50 years or so while many houses in Europe are kept for well over 100 years.

Humans generate large quantities of waste which today in western countries is collected and taken to landfills or dumps. The waste then sits there to rot and disintegrate for long periods of time, maybe for several hundred years. These dumps are usually covered when they are full and used for recreational purposes. There has been some recognition that this primitive method is inefficient and, to coin a phrase, "wasteful." It was realized that the decaying waste generates methane gas which is harmful if dissipated into the atmosphere, so they have started to devise ways for its collection. This involves installing large inverted funnels in the garbage pits to collect the gas and transfer it to the natural gas pipeline. (Natural gas is also Methane). This is a good start, but the objective is to have a zero waste and utilize all garbage without tying up land indefinitely. By an extension of the collectables program being used today, this can be achieved and allow each segment to be disposed of in the most appropriate way. The biodegradables can be segregated and used for generating energy and collectables can be reused after meltdown or other processing. These include materials such as plastics, paper, cans and glass. Also, residue byproducts of meltdown processing can be used for road-making base materials.

Noise Pollution- Noise is a form of pollution seldom talked about because almost all noise is generated by oil based fuels being burnt in internal combustion engines which are a generally accepted part of life. But when a replacement for oil, based on renewable materials, comes into being, it will be coincidental with the introduction of fuel celled vehicles. These are basically electric vehicles with cells on the vehicle generating electricity to feed the motor. They are virtually silent and will progressively take over all internal combustion engine vehicles and equipment. These include cars, trucks, motor cycles, construction and farm equipment, lawn mowers and weed whackers and, one day, even aircraft. It will create a condition of no noise pollution. The only disappointment is that the change will take many years to accomplish. Ironically, the first batches of new electric cars are just hitting the market, and the biggest concern with them is that they cannot be heard in the street. There is talk that they may be required to have beeping units to give warning of their presence.

The world has to redirect itself towards a more rationalized and sustainable existence which will reduce pollution and provide for a more pleasant environment for the world's inhabitants. The progressive change back from non-renewable to renewable-based products will involve many upsets in the process and take time to achieve.

Chapter 7

WHAT ACTUALLY TRIGGERED THE RECESSION-DEPRESSION

America has led itself, and consequently the world, into a mire of economic and industrial disarray which could rival the great depression of 1929. The start of this horrendous demise is being attributed to the crash of the U.S. housing market. This is a true statement, but what caused the housing market to crash is an interesting and important issue.

It was initiated by the dramatic impact of 9/11 in 2001, causing a wave of general uncertainty and insecurity and because of the Arab association, started the price of oil on a dramatic upward curve. The price of oil was again boosted in 2002 with the start of the Iraq war.

At the time of 9/11 the price of oil was $21 a barrel which quickly increased to over $100 a barrel by 2008. In the period from 2003-2005 the oil price increase impacted the economy with the Real Cost of Living (COLA) rising dramatically. This was mainly due to the radical increase in the cost of transportation which is a most consequential segment in the total price of all items and activities. Particularly hard-hit was the construction industry which has extremely high transportation content in both its operations and the materials it uses. Consequently, the industry, including new house construction, started to slow down substantially in 2006. This, in turn, impacted the over-heated used house market and uncovered the sub prime mortgage issue which caused the whole housing market bubble to burst and uncover further deficiencies existing in the financial systems.

This, coupled with the still increasing COLA and the high price of gasoline at the pump, led to sparking the recession and destabilizing the U.S. and worlds economies by causing a massive financial crisis, all triggered by the oil price escalation as shown in Figure 12 and huge amounts of money being drained from the financial system each day.

As previously stated, oil was discovered in the mid-1800's and initially used as a fuel for lamp lighting, but it was soon displaced by electricity which was cleaner, safer and more convenient. Toward the end of the 19th century, oil found another application as fuel for the newly invented internal combustion engine. This form of propulsion rapidly became the powering choice for all the new forms of mechanical transportation that were emerging including cars, trucks, aircraft, shipping, farm machinery, military, mobility and construction equipment and a host of other pieces of equipment and machinery which required their source of fuel to accompany the machine. Oil speeded up the final stages of the industrial revolution, and transportation was an essential and major

THE RECESSION/DEPRESSION

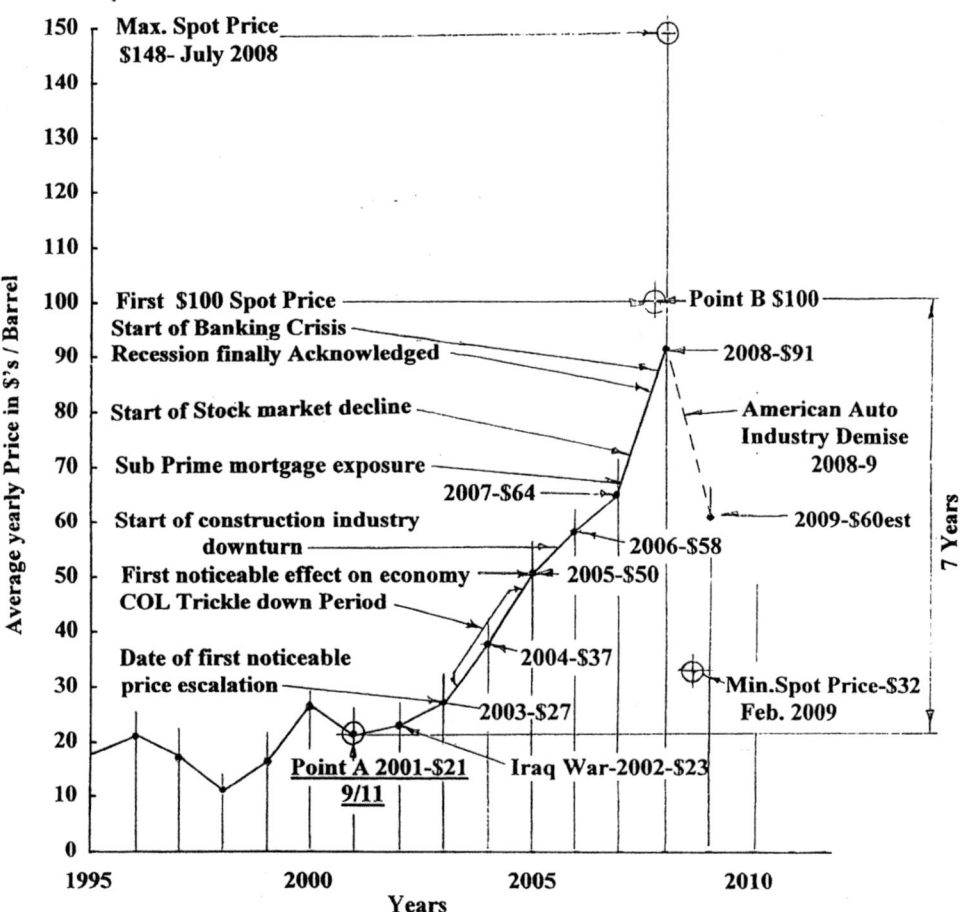

Figure 12 : *Oil Price Escalation and its effect on the Economy 2001-2010*

part of developing building and maintaining the Wondrous World of Comfort and Convenience the Western World lives in today. Oil was also the commodity that allowed the change from mixed farming to mass producing crops in one area and shipping them extensive distances in air conditioned trucks to the market place.

From the beginning of oil's usage, it was recognized to be a fossil-based fuel and, consequently, nonrenewable or sustainable. This important factor was ignored, however, as oil's availability seemed endless. America itself had sufficient oil beneath its territories to supply its own needs until the 1960s. But today the United States imports some 70% of the 24 million barrels per day which is the amount it consumes in normal circumstances. This is some 25% of the world's total usage of approximately 94 million barrels a day even though U.S.'s population is only 300 million or about 5% of the world's total population of some 6.4 billion. (The Recession has caused a temporary reduction in oil's usage because of the general slowdown in the world's development activities).

Oil has now reached a point where supply is only just meeting demand, and in a few years, this balance will only be made by progressively increasing availability of a renewable replacement for oil. Meantime, America is dependant on the foreign oil imports. If the world's known oil reserves are extrapolated at projected usage rates, there is enough oil left to last for some 50 years. But as Sheikh Zaki Yamani, the then head of OPEC, philosophized in the 1970's, **"The Stone Age did not end for lack of stone and the Oil Age will end long before the world runs out of oil!"** People think 50 years seems a long time and often comment, "Why should I worry because it's beyond my lifetime." This "debate ending" remark is somewhat akin to Andy Warhol's comment, "That I am not afraid of death but I just don't want to be there when it happens."

Since the 1960's, all presidential election debates have promised to *free America from its dependence on foreign oil.* However, at the end of each political reign, the percent of oil which is imported has escalated because the government has not initiated an appropriate conservation program. Conservation is a difficult issue to approach politically because it is almost impossible to deal with effectively without imposing some vote jeopardizing hardship on the public. Now however, the resulting financial crisis and economic recession is forcing a reaction to the subject.

The responsibility for allowing the oil situation to deteriorate and jeopardize the economy can be blamed on the government for not initiating a meaningful conservation program and not highlighting the need for development of a renewable replacement for oil. But the American automotive industry is the real culprit for allowing it to happen. Their greed factor to enhance profits by producing large, inefficient gas guzzling vehicles loaded with a multitude of expensive options, at a time when there was a need for producing more basic less expensive more efficient smaller vehicles to suite the bad economic times, is deplorable. The industry blames it on the customers because they say, "That is what the public were demanding." With this philosophy, it is understandable that as the recession has progressed, it has almost put the American automobile industry out of business.

As stated, it was the escalating price of oil which initiated the oil crisis which then progressed through the construction industry downturn, the housing market crash, the sub- prime mortgage exposure, the start of the stock market decline and the whole chain of events leading to the financial crisis and the world economic downturn as shown in Figure 12.

At the time of 9/11, the price of a barrel of oil was $21 which cost the U.S. Economy approximately **$.5 billion a day**. At $60 a barrel, the cost to the economy was nearly **$1.5 billion a day**, and at $100 a barrel that cost rose to nearly **$2.5 billion per day** of which 70% goes to overseas sources. It was these horrendous daily costs which, together with the ongoing expense of the Iraq and Afghanistan wars, combined with the sub-prime mortgage debacle were the main factors which uncovered the banking system weakness and failures. This, in turn, caused the financial crisis that culminated in the deep economic recession that the world is now experiencing.

In the 2008-9 period, the price of oil temporarily rose to $148 then, because of the crisis, dropped substantially to a spot price of $32 a barrel. However, it soon rose again to over $70 a barrel and is still climbing. The implications of this will only be fully defined when the new global usage rate and the demand for oil is re-established and stabilized. The people are naturally happy that the price of fuel at the pump is now around $2-2.6 a gallon, and consequently, the cost of living is reduced. The flip side of this, however, is that the reduced price of oil is a byproduct of the world's activity level slowing down which in turn is fueling the recession still further. The demand and price of oil are the main economic indicators determining the length and depth of the recession. When the price stops falling, it will signal the bottom of the recession; when it starts rising again, it will indicate that world development activities are restarting. Because oil supply has temporarily caught up with demand, some people have stopped believing that there is an oil problem. But, we have to reduce the amount of oil we use because, even if it was available, we cannot afford it; at $80 per barrel it costs the economy some **$700 billion dollars a year.** This is the same huge amount that was demanded and approved in 2008 as a one time payment to prevent a financial system meltdown.

The new American administration with its philosophy of "Change" is a welcome presence for taking on the whole set of the U.S. and world's major problems simultaneously. Unfortunately, they are taking control at a time when the world situation has deteriorated to an unbelievably low level. Fortunately, however, they have recognized the need to proceed on a multi-front recovery program as the only rational way to have a reasonable chance to resolve the multitude of interrelated issues. The programs already launched should progressively correct most of the administration and management factors, but the all-important transportation fuel issue has not yet come into focus. Unfortunately, the present deteriorated economic situation is likely to continue until a renewable replacement for oil is in place to help stop the financial blood-letting and also resolve many of the outstanding oil related international political situations and the interrelated population, energy and environmental issues.

The World Depression was started in 2001 on 9/11 by a well-educated Arab living in a cave in the middle of Arabia. He must by now have a very satisfied smirk on his face for being able to create a World Crisis with a negligible amount of money but with some very cruel, devious but intelligent long-term planning. He must also be amused that the Western World, despite its huge resources, can't find or catch him. He blames the whole situation on America interfering in the Arab world involving a long string of events including: the Iraq war, the Kuwaiti war, America's support of Israel and other activities dating back to before the deposing of the Shah of Iran in 1979. Of course, one can also link all these events to the issue of oil.

Chapter 8

MANAGEMENT AND PLANNING

The rules of management and planning of world situations are similar to all normal programs which are based on gathering data- applying judgment of right and wrong and good and bad, sound logic and straight forward common sense from every point of view, including the effect of looking at issues from a point in the future. However, these rules are not easy to follow because they require us to stand back and refocus our thoughts and actions from a normal every day format to a basis where only the facts (truth) and unlimited time apply. This might seem straight forward, but we live in a world where we consciously or subconsciously make plans within our lifespan and converse and communicate to be socially and politically correct whether or not it may be the truth.

Little Johnny is taught at school not to say out loud, "Willie Smith has wet his pants," and little girls are taught to complement rather than criticize. All this leads to adults saying the right things to please which may not necessarily be accurate. It does, however, lead to a much more peaceful and pleasant society. Politically, one is not supposed to profile people by ethnic or religious implications and to be very careful how one interjects these factors into conversation. *This selective avoidance form of communication* has become normal practice and is often tainted with other feelings like sentimentality and desire which can generate "spin and hype" instead of facts.

The art of planning and programming worldwide long-term events outside one's lifespan is difficult from many aspects. There is always the temptation to consider pursuing only the short term most profitable and readily available solutions and to enjoy the good life while it lasts. This self-centered disregard for the long-term effect has led to, and will continue to lead to, some disastrous situations. When individuals or even corporations are planning, the timing base is usually the lifespan of the person or, in the case of a corporation, the expected time of a return on investment. This results in program duration of maybe up to 20 years. This is in contrast to world issues which are sometimes relatively short but mostly involve much longer terms like several human generations and even hundreds of years or more.

Managing and planning global issues on a world wide basis is a formidable challenge, and before embarking on considerations of the myriad of permutations and combinations involved, it is worth fantasizing to help appreciate the size and implications of the problem at hand:

The setting can be considered the world as a stage with the general public as the audience while the arena is filled with many and varied participants who are trying to piece together a jigsaw puzzle of horrendous proportions. There are masses of groups including scientists, inventors, engineers, physicists, academics, lawyers, businessmen, corporations, bankers, product planners, religious leaders and, of course, politicians.

The game and spectacle of putting the massive jigsaw puzzle together is different from any other game or problem solving the world has previously witnessed. For example, none of the players or spectators who start the game will be there to witness the completion as they will progressively and continually be replaced over a period of indeterminable length but certainly over hundreds and maybe even thousands of years. The Timekeeper - Referee is Father Time who stands with a stop watch not graduated in minutes and seconds but in centuries.

The stadium is owned by the Almighty Creator of the world who lights the arena each morning with the sun and turns off the lights each night. He also provides sustenance and energy for the spectators and participants together with the materials and constituents for solving all the problems and subjects in the massive jigsaw puzzle.

Father Time starts the proceedings each day and patiently watches the antics and actions of all concerned. He observes the almost total lack of interest on the part of the audience who does not pay any attention unless something happens like World Wars, 9/11, an Iraq situation, global warming or an oil crisis. This is because most of the time the audience is preoccupied with the implications and pleasures of living in this Wondrous World of comfort and convenience that has been created for them.

Father Time regards the participants pursuing their activities including the politicians who repeatedly do their two and four year pirouettes like lightning bugs around a candle flame before falling to the floor to become minute specks on the pages of history. He also

It All Started With 9/11

watches the special interest groups trying to influence the activities without realizing that in this set of problems only honest answers will be meaningful as a final solution. He watches the thankful look of relief on the faces of some of the academics who know they will be long gone when their theories are finally judged. He sees the difficulty of keeping inventors and originators happy and enthusiastic in a political world and usually not living long enough to see the results of their efforts which is their normal reward for achievement. He looks at the corporate product planers with amusement because their idea of the long-term program is 5 to 10 years, and here they are now dealing with issues involving hundreds of years or more.

Father Time patiently continues to oversee the whole operation, and the puzzle building progresses, but there is always a large portion left for future generations to resolve---

When major world events are being discussed by the public, the debaters usually have not spent enough time away from enjoying this Wondrous World to think about or come up with any proposals or solutions and very often refuse to believe in the seriousness of the issues involved. They blindly think or hope that the government will sort things out, and their debate ending remarks in closing out a discussion on world problems are often, "Why should I worry because I won't be here when it happens," or, "If things are that bad somebody will come up with an answer."

Individuals cannot solve these massive world wide issues, and it's foolish to hope that private enterprise, in the form of corporations, will enter the arena and resolve issues by bringing market forces into play. It, therefore, becomes a governmental issue, but unfortunately governments are usually controlled by politicians who use a different timescale on which to reference their actions and decision-making. These include: How long is it to the next election? How long is the next term? How will an issue be received

Management and Planning

by the majority of the voting public? How is a given subject likely to be received by various religious, ethnic and other groups? And, most importantly, Will it be popular and generate votes? So, the response to a question often is based on its popularity and is influenced by party politics rather than based on logic or personal choice of the voting politician. Governments are also known to be slow- moving and inefficient, particularly when dealing with technical or complicated logistical issues, but on the other hand, they have been known to achieve great success with such projects as the moon program. So even with all their fault's and disadvantages, there is really no obvious alternative to governments handling the major world wide programs and problems.

The timing issue illustrated above with the Father Time fantasy is no exaggeration. Generally, people find it very difficult to think and plan outside their life span, and it is not natural for them to position themselves 50 or 100 years ahead when studying and considering long term decisions on current factors. The choice of the basic energy materials is a good example where ease of availability and a quick return on investment took precedence over the long-term negative effects. This resulted in such major energy choices as coal, oil and gas which are all non-renewable, non-sustainable materials having the detrimental affects of mining together with atmospheric pollution and global warming. This was in exchange for short term profit and convenience which typically draws the remark, "Well they won't run out in my lifetime." Consequently, we are now embroiled in all the resulting problems to resolve because of oil starting to run out, and coal and oil are causing severe detrimental effects to the environment of planet Earth together with playing a major part in causing the world economic crisis. Fortunately, when the decision is finally made and implemented on the renewable replacement material for oil to be used as transportation fuel, it will not only go a long way in resolving the energy supply problem but also affect many of the factors relating to the Population and Environmental issues.

- Firstly, when trying to resolve problems, it is first necessary to acknowledge that the problem exists.
- Secondly, it is essential to have an honest and accurate description of the problem with unbiased inputs, free of hype, sentiment and desire.
- Thirdly, the solution must conform to the rules of sustainability including the choice of the materials being renewable and having only totally recyclable waste.

SO WHERE ARE WE?
HOW DID WE GET HERE?
HOW BAD IS IT?
CAN ANYBODY DO ANYTHING ABOUT IT?

So where are we?

We have been living in a fool's paradise where people believed that the wondrous world we live in would go on forever. The fact that the foundation of this wonderful life was largely based on non-renewable materials, and therefore non-sustainable, was ignored and not talked about. That the Western World's business and political systems had been left to run on "Human Trust" without checks and balances, was incredible. This was combined with uncontrolled deficit spending instead of paying as you go. The public and politicians thought that we were safe and secure because we have the largest Gross Domestic Product (GDP) in the world and the mightiest military force the world has ever seen.

How did we get here?

The decay in "Our way of life" started a long time ago when we commenced planning for the present without regard for the long-term future, and the total system just received a final eight year set-back because of unqualified leadership.

How bad is it?
The result is we are now in a deep recession that, because of its momentum, could develop into a depression. But the pundits will tell you that that's not possible because we don't have guidelines for such a thing.

Can anybody do anything about?
Yes! Fortunately, the new administration is doing exactly what it should. The situation is so bad you can't pick and choose issues to tackle. Everything is so interrelated you can only tackle the whole spectrum of factors at once. Because of the nature of the problem it will take many "trial and error" attempts to resolve it. Unfortunately, this will give the political opposition plenty of opportunities to be disparaging at a time when unity of purpose is called for. This generates a thought for the future when government systems will need to be reviewed. The problem is made even more complex because domestic issues cannot be prioritized over international events. This is because America's weight and impact is crucial to a large portion of the world. This just increases the size of the task at hand.

It's been known from the beginning that unemployment would be the crucial issue. A natural byproduct of the slumping business sector culminates in letting people go onto the unemployment rolls. There will also be a lag in time after businesses start to recover before the employment issue will improve. Meanwhile, the political detractors keep shouting from the sidelines that, "The plan is not working." The stimulus package on one hand and the cleansing of business systems on the other will eventually pay-off.

Be considerate and patient because there is no other alternative. The days of pandering to the rich in the hopes of it trickling down to the less rich are gone.

Chapter 9

SUSTAINABILITY

As previously stated, the world was created with a fully sustainable system for its existence and survival with the sun providing all the needs for the animal and vegetable life on its surface. Any waste generated was completely recycled back into the system which created a "Dust to Dust" self-supporting circle of events which is known as "Nature's Way."

This total system of sustainability existed and continued until a few hundred years ago when mankind discovered non-renewable materials which he could mine from the earth's surface and use to improve his standard of living. This reduced the World's Sustainability period to that of the supply lifespan of these non-renewable materials. It also started to generate large quantities of non-recyclable waste, caused air pollution, and the mining involved degrading large areas of the Earth's surface. The non-renewable materials varied greatly in their time of likely availability, but this was not considered a concern as their estimated end points were mostly beyond a human's lifespan.

However, now some of these critical non-renewable commodities, to which humans have become addicted, have usage rates which are starting to exceed supply. The first major commodity in this category is **oil** which is the fuel powering the all-important World's Transportation System. It has become the base fuel for the internal combustion engines which have been used in all forms of automotive transportation, and other machinery, for over 100 years. But the work on developing a replacement for oil derived from a renewable base material has not, until recent years, been brought to the general public's attention: The debate on the factors surrounding ethanol has given some insight to the issue, but many people still don't understand that the need for a replacement and the reason for its price escalation are because **oil is running out.**

In general, it is not realized that the oil replacement situation is playing a major roll in generating the world economic recession which could degenerate into a depression to equal the great depression of 1929. This situation can be blamed on the lack of control by governmental systems which have largely relied on market forces to resolve issues. They are, consequently, based on manufacturers choosing approaches for short-term profits. This often ignores long-term effect, particularly when the periods of time involved are outside the human lifespan.

As previously stated, the start of the World Financial Crisis is largely being blamed on sub-prime mortgages and excesses in the deficit spending system causing the housing market to crash. Further review, however, reveals that what triggered the construction industry's crash in 2006-7 were the unstable times and the COLA escalating together with the horrific number of dollars that were being siphoned from the U.S. economy due to the price of oil escalating.

Sustainability

The world needs to return to a sustainable existence, and it can only do this by returning to Nature's Way. This is the same cycle of events that achieves sustainability for continuing our existence on planet Earth. Its process is based on using sun-based renewable crops and nature's ongoing continuous cycles of air, water, hydro, wind, solar, geothermal, warmth and light, etc.

We have already learned how to use Nature's Way for generating the sustenance (food) for our human existence; now we have to progressively plan on using its principles for generating everything else we need. This is because all non-renewables by definition will eventually disappear. We also have to achieve this objective by "total usability" without creating or generating any waste that can't be recycled back into nature's cycle. If we abide by the sustainability rules of using only renewables, the zero waste issue will largely look after itself. The actions will also have to be achieved without unduly damaging the Earth's surface or polluting its atmosphere.

The implications of growing everything we need are enormous. However, any deep thinking discussion will quickly reveal that there are no other candidates for sustainability without relying on magical gadgets or science fiction type miracles, i.e., the National Ignition Facility which is now reportedly complete and relates to the possibility of utilizing the Sun's Fusion Process

Fortunately, wood, which is the most enduring of materials, has been a principal provider for our existence from the beginning of time and continues to exist and flourish. The trees have sustained themselves despite assaults by mankind, and they, together with other vegetation, will become the central supplier for our future needs. This includes energy, and it will be the means of changing back from an industrial to an agricultural society.

When analyzing or studying the World's major problems under the three main categories of Population, Energy and Environmental, the following factors emerge:

- They all have long-term timing implications beyond the human lifespan.

- Their resolution will eventually involve all of mankind's material needs being derived from recyclable crops which will require a change back from an industrial to an agricultural Economy?

- The problems are largely global with no country limits and, therefore, have to be resolved internationally.

- The oil replacement issue was one of the principal factors that triggered the world recession but most surprisingly, resolving the transportation fuel issue will also resolve a large portion of the other major problems the world is facing because they have interrelated common denominator solutions. For example: The necessity of growing all of mankind's needs will involve extending the usage of the world's land for agriculture. This will particularly include the under-utilized lands in the less developed countries, i.e., Africa. This, in turn, will provide the much-needed employment and, consequently, education opportunities which are necessary to solve the population problem in these countries. The transportation energy solution of replacing oil with a renewable crop will remove a principle contributor to the environmental pollution issue; additionally, the extended use of wind, solar, geothermal, etc, for progressively replacing coal to solve the general energy equation will greatly reduce environmental contaminants. Discontinuing the use of oil will also remove the biggest toxic ingredient in the world's business and political arenas.

- It should be remembered that when discussing sustainability, it is imperative to have accurate facts without the influence of fantasy, sentiment, desires and spin and hype.

- It should also be remembered that if an issue or situation is deemed inevitable, then plan for it.

The massive exercise of growing all that we use will require every available piece of land. It's interesting to note that in the Economist paper dated 23 May 2009 there were two interesting articles titled: "Buying Farmland Abroad." page 16 and "Land Deals in Africa" pages 61-63. These articles describe transactions which are going on between governments, not private individuals, and involve buying or renting large slices of land throughout the world. It states that the purpose is for growing staples or biofuels and pieces of land the size of France are being transacted. No doubt, China and the Arab states have also rationalized the land resource issue for their survival.

Chapter 10
THE AMERICAN AUTOMOBILE INDUSTRY

The American auto industry's lack of forward planning and failure to anticipate the effect of such issues as oil availability or a depressed economy is only the end of a long string of detracting activities that have been manifesting themselves since World War II. Prior to the war the, American industry was highly regarded and respected not only for its mass production technology, but also vehicle innovations. Providing the allied forces with the whole range of military equipment to win WW II was an example of the capability and generosity of the industry and country. In the post war period GM was again predominant in vehicle manufacturing with plants throughout the world and was by far the largest manufacturer. Ironically, a principal worry of GM was not to exceed the 51% anti-trust production limit in America. Unfortunately, America has now lost the product and manufacturing leadership to Japan, Asia and Europe.

During the 1950's and 1960's America produced some of the most incredible automobiles ever invented. They were mostly huge, outlandish monsters with nonfunctional styling features that made them as aerodynamic as a brick. These models were replaced or dramatically face lifted on a yearly basis, and they were powered by oversized engines that drank the $.30 a gallon gas as though there was no tomorrow. They were light-years apart from the models originally produced by Henry Ford which were designed to get you from A to B economically and only came in the color black. These new monsters came in all colors of the rainbow, the louder the better including "Titty Pink," and some were in two and three tones. They were also adorned by more chrome than a movie house entrance, and as far as quality was concerned, it was as if the word had not been invented. There were brief flashes of normality with some small cars from AMC and the imported Volkswagen Bug that generated a following. It was a time when so-called styling was dominant above all else, and there was competition between manufacturers to generate the next most outlandish styling feature. GM was usually the leader, and if the industry spy system said they were going to have bigger fins or wrap around windshields, the others would go into a panic and try to be there at the same time. There was only minor interest in what was under the skin except to make sure that there was plenty of horse power and to popularize such happenings as automatic transmissions and air conditioning as prominent sales features.

This situation existed until the 1970's when new product standards were established by the Japanese industry for quality, reliability, price, efficiency and emission controls. They also responded to the progressive demise of oil with conservation product design direction, i.e., hybrids. These actions resulted in the Japanese and other Asian manufacturers becoming the world's leaders in producing and marketing automotive vehicles. Meanwhile, the American automotive industry has pursued what might be likened to one last drunken party before oil's demise will completely reduce the American and the world's economies to shambles. The course chosen by the American industry of bigger, more powerful gas guzzling vehicles could not have been more contrary to the present market's needs or the future. The American industry, led by GM, is now on bended knee trying to persuade the American government to provide financial and administrive support at a time when the country is already bleeding to death financially.

In the ensuing years American vehicles went through several phases of change including the initial downsizing in response to the fuel shortages of the 1970's and becoming more aerodynamic and of improved quality, aimed at the standards set by the Japanese manufacturers. But their Style Dominated Dynasty has continued and has become even more ingrained in their culture, and the vehicles' functional operating systems are still issues that are largely taken for granted.

Meanwhile, the functional requirements of transportation need extensive redesign innovation to run on renewable based fuels to replace oil and be smaller, more efficient and less expensive in order to meet economically depressed times. The overseas competition has responded to many of these challenges while the American industry is still in the "Style Dominated Groove" and has not, until recently, even anticipated the oil crisis.

The result is that two of the Big-Three have gone through bankruptcy, and the third is losing large sums of money. Meanwhile, world competition has reacted to the approach of oil's demise and has for several years produced radically new types of drive systems such as hybrids as an interim conservation measure. Toyota has now passed GM to become the world's largest automobile manufacturer and has become the market share leader. The Big Three have claimed that their problem is employee benefit expense that the competition doesn't have. But, even if the American companies dumped all their benefit responsibility on the government, they would still not be competitive. Their misguided management practice of prioritizing Style over Function to gain product leadership is inherently wrong. This is particularly true in an era where highly technical capability is required to invent vehicles for the post oil-age so as to meet the World Crisis.

The Big-Three have also followed a misconception that the oil crisis is many years away and have not, until more recently, shown any great interest in conservation models such as smaller vehicles and hybrids. Also, the industry has not even considered the economy deteriorating into a deep recession, and neither the industry nor the administration has made any meaningful attempt at a conservation program.

What's more, two years ago GM and Ford announced that they were realigning their organizations to put the designers- they used to be called Stylists- in charge of the all-important product development. However, the people needed to invent and develop new concepts like hybrids and fuel cell cars are highly creative technical engineers, not artists. They still don't get it that the only good Inventor-Artist we ever knew was Leonardo De Vinci--and that *form follows function*, and that's why air planes can fly----

Their only hope now is for the American manufacturers to be taken over by new, experienced management teams who will place priority emphasis on the correct type of vehicles and their functional vehicle systems and make styling a very important, but, taken for granted factor. Because such teams do not exist domestically any more, partnerships will have to be negotiated with overseas corporations. The Chrysler-Fiat arrangement is an excellent example of what should happen to GM and Ford. The two companies that are obvious candidates for such arrangements are Toyota and Honda.

Realizing the magnitude and importance of the program to determine a replacement for oil from a renewable source should stimulate an aggressive development effort similar to that generated for World War II or the moon project. It will require inputs from a variety of engineers including, mechanical, electrical, chemical, hydraulic, agriculture, manufacturing and even sanitation all orchestrated by automotive engineers. It would normally be assumed that our automotive industry would be those responsible to meet this challenge. Unfortunately, because of their ingrained "Style and Sales for immediate profit culture" and their lack of realistic long-term planning and not even being able to anticipate the current oil situation and the associated economic down turn, they have disqualified themselves from being appropriately qualified. Recently, GM's top product executive has conceitedly stated that, "GM gives the public what they desire, and if they want big cars, GM will produce them." He has also openly stated global warming is a crock of s--t and has downplayed the need for fuel saving models such as hybrids. When one hears this, one can understand why GM's product lines are totally unsuitable for the current market: They will not even meet the government's fuel requirements for 2011, while the Japanese manufacturers already meet virtually all requirements for 2015. GM's philosophy is prevalent with both Ford and Chrysler but to different degrees. None of them have realistically anticipated or reacted to oil's demise either by a conservation program or a renewable replacement for oil or that the change over would be at a time of an economic downturn.

It is obvious that the American automotive industry needs a complete re-vamping starting with a clean sheet and most likely to be managed by a foreign corporation selected from the existing world leaders. To financially support the old management and their out of date philosophies and practices will only continue to produce uncompetitive models. Also, using civil servants to oversee management will not design and develop products with leadership capability. A totally new start needs to be made with no carry over encumbrances such as unions and other benefits systems such as health and pensions which will, hopefully, be part of the general social system in the future.

The controlled sale of Chrysler to Fiat is most probably the best thing that could have happened. It automatically brings a whole range of small cars into the equation and has the positive possibility that the Fiat management team may be capable of injecting the correct product development philosophy that the company needs. The problem now is to find or conjure up a similar arrangement for the reconstituting of GM. This would involve a similar sale; some ownership arrangement whereby a Toyota or Honda will take over GM with their own skilled management team. Unfortunately, the old GM team is in charge of organizing the new GM structure and, unbelievably, one of their first actions is to re-appoint the old head of product development who caused their present diabolical situation. It's discouraging to think of the once great American auto industry's markets being taken over by the Japanese and other overseas manufacturers but unless there is radical management and organizational changes in the U.S. companies, they will fail.

Solving the replacement of oil problem with a new fuel material derived from a renewable source is the cornerstone to the world's future. It not only resolves the transportation issue but also many other major problems because it's certainly going to necessitate generating a massive agricultural expansion for growing the renewable source material. This action could provide occupational involvement in many of the under developed countries consequently helping to solve the education and population problems. It would also be a tremendous help with environmental issues and with sustainability in general. It would also resolve many of the ongoing international disputes and conflicts which have oil as their underlying cause.

If the suggested corporate partnerships don't materialize, then it might be necessary to resort to the "Skunk Works" approach. Which, as stated, has been used to solve complicated problems involving many complex issues has successfully been accomplished by setting up a small group as a "Skunk Works", i.e., Ford Anglia 105E, Ford Cardinal Study, Ford GT 40, Jeep XJ Cherokee, AMC 4WD Eagle, Renault E Car Study, etc. This could operate under governmental and national security auspices for gathering state-of-the-art information and material to establish program direction. This is an approach which has been used many times in many industries for resolving complicated invention issues. This would have been much easier 20 or 30 years ago when this capability still existed in the U.S. industry, but the style-controlled management evolution in recent years has now made this type of free thinking individual or group a dying breed.

The present oil fueled internal combustion engine automotive vehicles have evolved over a period of more than 100 years. They now need totally new vehicle design configurations to meet changing economic times, the demise of oil, the need to change to fuel-cells and to run on a new pump-fuel derived from a renewable base material. This provides a great opportunity for ingenuity of not only redesigning the power source, but all other vehicle systems including; suspensions, drive lines, wheels, tires, seating, controls, etc. The objective should be to re-establish the American automotive industry, with overseas help, to a position of product leadership by designing and developing much more efficient and basic vehicles while resolving the oil replacement issue. This in turn will go a long way to solving the world recession.

Never has the need for **Change** been more appropriate!

Chapter 11
FUTURE TRANSPORTATION FUELS AND VEHICLES

The lack of realistic long-term planning has largely been responsible for generating the ongoing **World Crisis** because such critical items as **running out of oil** have been virtually ignored. Also, the American automobile companies have gone on producing large, costly, inefficient vehicles loaded with options on the assumption that the economy would continue at its "Alice in Wonderland" magical level, and they could continue reaping their high profits.

Meanwhile, a large portion of the developing world is trying to create vehicles that will allow them to graduate from a bicycle and a powered rickshaw. But, unfortunately, they've followed the developed world's lead by propelling them with oil based fuel. To any reasonable, deep-thinking individual, the "oil age" has to end sometime, and the change to a new fuel would cause a mighty economic upheaval even if we had prepared for it by developing a renewable replacement for oil. As the decision on a renewable fuel has not been made, the upheaval level will be so much greater and the available time factor for a solution made shorter.

Europe and much of the world have developed smaller vehicles because they have taxed fuel oil heavily resulting in about $8 per gallon at the pump. This has had the effect of generating smaller, more efficient vehicles, but even these are still not efficient enough to make oil last until a new fuel is available. Due to this situation, there are three essential factors to be responded to:

- Firstly, it is necessary to introduce all appropriate conservation measures and to progressively raise the price of gasoline until it is roughly equivalent to that of Europe in order to persuade individuals to buy efficient vehicles and, conversely, to effectively induce the manufacturers to produce them.

- Secondly, it is essential that manufacturers bring to the market place as quickly as possible basic, inexpensive, four seat vehicles that are the most efficient and cost effective alternatives possible. They should focus on using existing non-exotic materials in their construction, and a version of the vehicle should be available, stripped of its non-essentials.

- There will still be some larger vehicles for those who can afford to run them. But the primary aim should be to encourage the manufacture and usage of smaller much more efficient vehicles. Meaningful fuel conservation will not be attained by trying to improve the efficiency of large vehicles.

- Thirdly, it is essential that the decision be made regarding the selection of the source material for the new fuel to replace oil and programs for its production and processing to be instigated. This will enable the design and development of fuel cell vehicles to be accelerated.

Conservation- Even if all the administration's business plans being developed work as expected, the period we are entering into has to be very much worse because of the directional inertia that has built up. The unemployment issue alone would seemingly assure this. Although not wanting to arouse unnecessary concern, the author needs to be realistic in order to make appropriate recommendations for the transportation and fuel of the future. He is also speaking from experiencing such events having lived through the 1929 depression in Europe where he remembers seeing people tightening their belts and throwing up in the street because of hunger. Setting the targets and objectives too low will not help!

It is also not practical or appropriate to ask the public what they want or would accept in a future car because their answers will change considerably after they have been through two or three years of deep recession with its associated devaluation of their financial resources. The conservation and environmental actions need to be harsh to jolt people into action, but they also need to be virtually immediate, not several years away. *The new rules also need to apply to existing vehicles not only to those yet to be built.*

There are many factors that fall into this immediate effect category of fuel conservation, i.e., speed limits, driving education, etc. But the most effective is increasing the price of gasoline at the pump. This is unfortunate because price is the most difficult issue to deal with politically, but its range of effects is enormous. It automatically dispenses with the need for the mpg laws and the un-necessary expense of applying and monitoring them, and it minimizes cheating. It automatically helps to educate the public on what they can afford and induces those that can afford it to buy more efficient vehicles which will provide the much needed activity at the auto plants. It also defines for the manufacturer what will sell and also becomes an effective source of revenue for the administration. Ironically, the price of gasoline will automatically increase rapidly again as the world activities recommence and market forces alone could increase the price to the $8 level. Already, in the first four months of 2009, the price of a barrel of oil has risen from a low of $32 to over $70. The logic of increasing pricing ahead of the true market cost will need some very skillful selling by the administration, and it will have to be introduced on a progressive basis.

The new four seat economic basic car- The definition of what this might be varies among individuals and depends on what's available in the marketplace and, very importantly, the prevailing economic climate which in turn depends on the degree and depth of the economic recession. Some people think that a Cadillac fitted with a hybrid driveline qualifies. Also, there are now some smaller vehicles in the Big Three's offerings which would be considered small vehicles by present day standards. These, however, are far from the levels of fuel economy and price that are likely to be required for the basic car of the future. Some of the so-called "B" segment imports such as Toyota Yaris and the Honda Fit are in the right direction but are still not quite there. The real answers are in vehicles such as the Toyota iQ and the Nano from the Tata Company in India because of their efficiency and price. See Figure 13.

The recently announced fuel efficiency requirements established by the Administration produced an interesting response from the U.S. auto industry. Their reply was that it would cause a substantial increase in price of the vehicles. This indicates how wrongly they deduce situations. In actual fact, the new requirements should reduce costs by changing the customer's choice of vehicle not only to a smaller size but to less expensive and more efficient models. They still have not understood that the most important factor for improving fuel economy is size and weight. We have to downsize like the rest of the world and get back to the basics of a vehicle's purpose which is to get you from A to B. Putting a hybrid engine in a Cadillac is only a psychological pacifier for someone's conscience.

Figure 13

The modern automobile has become the second most expensive item that an individual will ever purchase. The initial purchase plus its ongoing costs for fuel, service, insurance and frequency of replacing can even bring the overall cost of personal transportation to an unduly high level in lifetime purchases. Also, when a person's expenses against income are itemized, the line item for a car or cars is a major factor. All this brings up the issue of how basic is basic as applied to cars?

A car's original purpose, as stated, was to get the occupants and luggage from A to B. To this you can add to do it with reasonable comfort and speed and to do it in an enclosed weather-protected cabin. Over the past hundred years the definition of what should be included in a car has grown to an unbelievable level with a massive list of optional equipment and gadgets. These include climate controls, navigation equipment, TV and radio with CD and tape deck's, communication devices with automatic message sending features and a mass of electronics including computers to move seats and windows, lock doors, adjust mirrors, control lights and, more recently, to even park the car. All this gear adds considerable weight and cost, and it's carried around all the time even though it is only used occasionally and in some cases for only a few seconds. The manufacturers love it. Their most hated person is a customer ordering a stripped down model.

The basic car is most probably best defined as an entry level vehicle that can be afforded by the average person or family. These have often been called people's cars and date back to the Model T Ford which, being made with interchangeable components, could be mass-produced relatively inexpensively. The Volkswagen in the 1930's was Hitler's answer to the people's transportation. The latest car to qualify in this category is the Nano which is being made in India by the Tata company and it's about to hit the market with a selling price of $2,500 in India. It is a cute looking little four seat car with a .6 L 35HP 2 cylinder engine mounted in the rear and a four speed manual transmission. It has a single windshield wiper and only one rear view mirror and only minimal other equipment; it is a huge step up from the scooters and motorized rickshaws it replaces, and it is reported to achieve something over 50 mpg. A somewhat more upgraded model is planned for the European market for introduction in 2011 and is reported to still cost less than $5,000. The modern automobile has become too expensive, and a Nano might be an interesting choice even in America.

The American market's smallest high volume cars at present are the Toyota Yaris and the Honda Kit which are both very acceptable little cars. But there is a new Toyota advanced car that was first shown last year and named the iQ model. It won the SAE best new car of 2009 award and is labeled a Microcar. It is a four seat, with a squeeze, and has a front wheel drive using a 1 L 3 cyl. engine and an automatic transmission and achieves over 50 mpg. This vehicle will most probably present the answer to the second essential factor at the beginning of this chapter and will become an industry benchmark, but its selling price at this stage is unknown.

<u>Fuel and the Car of the future</u>- In the early 1900's automobiles started to become the public's main means of personal transportation, and, amazingly, its basic format hasn't changed since that time. It consists of a body, which is a weatherproof cabin that houses the passengers and luggage, has four wheels with pneumatic tires, a range of chassis systems including suspension, steering, transmission and driveline and is powered by an internal combustion engine fueled by oil based products.

After over 100 years of refinement, today's automobiles are modern marvels of engineering. All their systems have been upgraded and developed to provide improved comfort and convenience for the occupants with once manually operated items now being powered by electric, pneumatic or hydraulic sources. In addition, a whole range of optional equipment is now available that lifts the comfort level to rival that of a well-appointed living room. However, four major issues have arisen that make it necessary to review the whole automotive design format:

- Oil is starting to run out which is escalating the price of fuel substantially.
- The world is in the grip of a deepening recession which makes it necessary to carefully review the cost of all items and particularly the cost of automobiles.
- Automotive emissions have now been recognized as a major contributor to destroying the Earth's climate.
- By necessity, we are being forced to progressively return to a system of sustainable living in order to continue existing.

Achieving answers to these issues is a huge undertaking, but the good news is that it gives the automotive creator a challenge and an opportunity to correct some of the fundamental negatives in the present automotive arrangement.

Despite the marvelous machine the modern automobile has become, it does have some major problems. They start with the internal combustion engine which is a noisy, inefficient, dirty operating machine. Apart from its noxious exhaust, it is the principal source of noise in the world. It has huge inherent efficiency losses, is expensive, heavy and complicated, and the fuel it presently uses is non-renewable. These negatives are in comparison to the electric motor which is clean and quiet and can be powered by fuel cells which run on renewable fuel.

The noise issue may seem unimportant at this stage because we have learned to tolerate and live with it. Go out and listen during the night, and despite the pleasant noises of nature, the principal noise will be traffic on neighboring roads or distant expressways, not to mention aircraft. During the day the traffic noise is joined by a chorus of lawn mowers, weed-whackers and other diabolically noisy IC engine machines like chain saws and pressure washers which can produce a high degree of discomfort. The anticipation of a world without ICE machines is a wonderful thought.

Fortunately, the one thing that finds general agreement by virtually everyone from academics to engineers is it that the vehicle of the future should be powered by an electric motor which is clean, quiet and efficient. The remaining debate, however, is over which category of electric propulsion it should use and, finally, what material the tank fuel should be for fuel-cell versions. Four possibilities are discussed below.

The true electric vehicle- This has an electric motor which is powered by on board rechargeable batteries. This arrangement has been used by commercial delivery vehicles back into the 1800's. Its limitations being the capacity of the batteries and the length of time it takes to recharge them. It's most suitable for applications where the vehicle usage is for a specific and known duration followed by a lengthy rest period during which the batteries can be recharged. The original applications were for daily deliveries of time sensitive materials such as ice and milk before the use of refrigeration and that were on a fixed route. More recently their use has been on golf carts and other applications with short duration journeys, followed by a lengthy rest period. Application to normal passenger cars has been limited because of the inconvenience of tailoring the usage time to the batteries' storage capacity and the recharging time. This first form of electric vehicle is now receiving considerably new production development with the advent of more efficient batteries such as lithium. Note: It should be remembered that this form of electric vehicle does require that its base form of electricity come from a plug-in charge. There are also subsystems being developed for more availability of plug-in opportunities while the owner is at work or shopping and also the possibility of shops or centers for complete battery exchange. This basic type of electric vehicle is already in limited production which is likely to increase with the renewed developments.

Second type of electric vehicle- This is essentially the same as the first approach but with the addition of an onboard small internal combustion engine to recharge the batteries if a plug in out-let is not available before the batteries are completely run down.

This approach is also receiving considerable development attention and is likely to start hitting the market within the next two years. This approach, however, is only a conservation measure opportunity as it still requires the use of a gasoline fueled internal combustion engine.

The well known hybrid approach- This uses an IC engine and an electric motor in unison by rationalizing their usage and optimizing their efficiencies by computer. There are now variations of this arrangement, i.e., the plug-in hybrid which adds a third contribution of household current when available. This approach is, again, only a conservation measure as it still relies on oil as the tank fuel.

A cautionary note! Many of the electric and hybrid vehicles depend on improved efficiency and reduce weight batteries. The favorite material for these new batteries is lithium which is a rare non-renewable metal. It is mainly mined from under salt flats, and Chile is presently the principal supplier followed by Australia and China. Up until the present its application has principally been for lap-top computers because of their requirement for light weight batteries which would hold an efficient charge. The drastic increase in usage for automobile applications is likely to create problems of supply and, consequently, price. It also has to be remembered that it is non-reviewable and does create high land degradation by mining. It is, therefore, not a long-term solution to the electricity storage problem.

The fourth arrangement is the highly desirable Fuel-cell-electric motor combination- This approach is virtually the first arrangement of a pure electric vehicle but with a so-called fuel-cell replacing the battery. The fuel-cell is a combination of a fuel container feeding a stack-cell device which chemically converts the fuel to electricity. There is general agreement that this fuel-cell and electric motor combination is what will be the power source for future vehicles to replace oil fueled ICE's. The only debate is what fuel should be in the tank to fuel the cell?

The Fuel for powering Fuel-Cells.

- A new base fuel to replace oil in the transportation system requires certain capabilities and characteristics:
- It must be renewable and, consequently, fully sustainable.
- It must have the capability to run a fuel-cell efficiently.
- It must be a safe fuel that can be easily transported, stored, dispensed and handled by the general public.
- It must also be available from existing sources and not be dependent on yet to be invented gadgets or processes, i.e., the recently completed National Ignition Facility with its fusion process.
- It is not essential, but it would avoid a huge logistical problem if it was also capable of powering existing IC engine vehicles with or without vehicle modifications, and it would simplify the distribution system.

There are three main candidates that have emerged from developments. They are:

Hydrogen — Methanol — Ethanol

<u>Hydrogen</u>- It is appropriate to review hydrogen first as it's the material that has received the most attention in the media. It is preferred by the academics because in many ways it is theoreti-

cally an ideal fuel. The politicians also like it because the label of a *Hydrogen Economy* has a nice promotional futuristic ring about it, but, unfortunately, it has some practicality problems.

Hydrogen exists in abundance in water (in combination with oxygen), but it does not exist in a free state. It can be separated out of water by electrolysis, and then it becomes a volatile gas. This has to be compressed to 5000 - 10,000 lbs. per square inch in order to store it in a reasonably sized fuel tank. It has been used extensively for rocket fuel in the space program where it is handled by specially equipped personnel. It is an ideal fuel to feed a fuel cell, and it can also be used in modified ICE vehicles where its exhaust is harmless steam. It takes large quantities of electricity for the electrolysis process. This is acceptable for a country like Iceland which has excesses of generated electricity because of its unique climate and topography providing large quantities of electricity from hydropower and geothermal sources. Producing the high quantities of electricity needed for electrolysis under normal circumstances would add to the already mammoth world problem of ceasing to use coal, oil and natural gas, all non-renewables, for electricity generation with the associated advantages of reduction in mining and emissions. Also, their proposal of sequestering underground the emission by-products is as unacceptable as sweeping the dog's droppings under the carpet.

An experienced vehicle designer will explain that selling vehicles to the public exemplifies Murphy's Law which states, **"If anything can go wrong, it will go wrong."** And one quickly learns that Schwartz's law follows which states, **"Murphy was an optimist."**

The general public has a considerable aptitude for inflicting pain and punishment on machinery which even the best engineering brains find intimidating. The vehicle engineer conspires with his testing department to set up a test program that will include every conceivable application known to man. It includes all industry procedures and factors the company has experienced in the past. Also, there are performance tests such as durability testing, crash testing, ride and handling testing and extreme climate testing along with a myriad of others carried out to the extremes of the imagination. But the general public always seems to find some new ways of causing problems. Therefore, the vehicle engineer has to resort to empirical judgments based almost on clairvoyance when considering new ideas.

A case in point is the subject of someone choosing hydrogen as the next base pump fuel. The experienced vehicle engineer will immediately shudder from tip to toe when he thinks of the general public handing it. He visualizes the diabolical issues that can arise from a fuel that has to be pressure stored in 5,000 to 10,000 psi containers in the hands of the "Glitch" generating public. Only a cloistered academic or a misguided politician could conjure up such an idea and think that it was feasible. This, coupled with the fact that hydrogen has to be manufactured by using fossil fuel for the foreseeable future with its emission by-products being buried in underground caverns, makes the whole proposal preposterous. This is not to say that hydrogen will not play a major part in the process, but using onboard reformers to derive it from another base fuel such as methanol or ethanol which would act, therefore, as a hydrogen carrier.

<u>Methanol-</u> CH_3OH is also called methyl wood alcohol, denatured alcohol or mentholated spirits. It is a colorless liquid at ambient conditions and is poisonous if ingested. It was originally produced by the dry distillation of wood, but today it is generated as a by-product of manufacturing ammonia, and it can also be derived from biomass.

It has been around seemingly forever for general home and industrial usage, and it is available from any hardware store. It has also been used as an automotive fuel in some areas and is noted for its use in racing cars such as the Indianapolis 500 vehicles where it was used between 1965 and 2007. It is obviously a high-energy fuel, and, like hydrogen, burns with an invisible flame, and, like gasoline, it is poisonous. If it were chosen as the next tank fuel, it may need additives to make the flame visible and the liquid bitter to taste. It would use basically the same transportation and dispensing equipment as used for gasoline but with selected material differences to avoid corrosion.

Ethanol- CH_3CH_2OH is also called ethyl alcohol or grain alcohol, and it is a colorless liquid at normal ambient conditions. It has been used since the 19th century as a solvent, disinfectant, preservative and an intoxicant in beverages, and it gained renewed attention in the fuel shortage of 1973. Essentially, it is an alcohol-based fuel generated by distilling and fermenting grain or other vegetation. It started to be used as an oxygenate additive to gasoline in the 1970's amid much controversy as to its technical contribution verses its political advantage of using surplus grain. Made from corn, it is a very inefficient product as it takes approximately 1 gallon of ethanol fuel to make 1.3 gallons of ethanol. Whereas the ethanol manufactured in Brazil from sugarcane generates 8 gallons for every gallon used in its production.

Ethanol could be a very important factor in the future oil replacement issue if only the corn lobby stopped over-promoting it and bad mouthing other candidates and if the implications of tax incentives and subsidies can be disentangled from its considerations of usage. Unfortunately, although suitable to replace oil in ICE engines, the nature of ethanol means that is not usually considered as a likely fuel for fuel cells.

A whole range of fuel cells using a variety of ingredients and for different purposes have emerged from development. The one that is favored for light vehicle applications is the proton exchange membrane fuel cell (PDMFC) which operates between 50-80°C and runs with an efficiency range of 50-60% and uses a polymeric membrane as an electrolyte. These units can run on hydrogen or with methanol used as a carrier together with a reformer. Direct acting methanol fuel cells DMFC are also under development which would also become candidates if successful.

All the electric, hybrid and fuel cell arrangements discussed provide the vehicle engineer with the opportunity for incorporating new features. With their electric drive motors, which are combined with a generator, they can be used in breaking not only to slow down the vehicle but to collect the power generated in deceleration. This is called regenerative braking and can eventually be integrated to replace the existing mechanical braking system which totally wastes the deceleration energy. The energy collected can be stored in the battery and used in conjunction with another feature which is called "zero speed idle shut off." Electrically driven vehicles automatically shut off at zero speed unlike present-day vehicles which waste fuel by idling in traffic lines and other hold ups. The vehicle does however need to use the restart capability more often, and, of course, heating and air conditioning still have to be supported during the temporary shutoff periods. This puts an extra load on the battery which should be partially offset by the regenerative breaking input.

When the decision is made on the choice of renewable material to produce the fuel to replace oil, the vehicle engineers can go to work. They will then have the basics for setting down the concepts to generate a fuel-cell car of the future. Fortunately, there have been some positive activities while all the vacillating regarding hydrogen has been running out the meter. These include vehicle systems that the advent of the "Electric Motor Propulsion" age make possible. The Internal Combustion Engine had limited choices as to its location in the vehicle package, but the electric motor opens up new and interesting possibilities. For example, an attractive choice is to locate the Electric-Motors -Come -Generates in the wheels. This dispenses with the need of having the heavy, noise and vibration generating mechanical drive-lines and transmissions of today's vehicles. A good example is what the Michelin Company has developed and calls an Active-Wheel. This includes not only the wheel and tire but also inside it is the motor-generator unit, an electrically operated suspension and the braking system. This combined set of major systems is electrically controlled and includes all aspects of ride, handling, braking and traction factors.

One can easily visualize the compact basic car of the future having these composite units in each of its two rear wheels. This simplifies and reduces the weight of all mechanical systems and components, i.e., the steering would be manual and not powered which is made possible by the lightness of the vehicle. Also, the steering linkage will be simplified by not having to articulate it with the suspension. This arrangement also allows the maximum freedom for packaging the structure- the heating-ventilating-cooling (HAVAC) systems, the passengers, luggage and the all important fuel cell and fuel tank.

Another feature which adds strength, saves weight, reduces cost and adds to safety is the fixed seat adjustable control arrangement. This is used in many racing car designs and also on golf carts.

A much-needed feature in the new basic car of the future is "All-Around-Protection." Today the public pays large amounts of money for a shiny new vehicle only to visit the supermarket and have a neighboring parked vehicle's door open against it and create hundreds of dollars of damage. All-Around-Protection minimizes this condition and can also be an important part of crash safety.

To reduce weight and cost, it will be necessary to dispense with many of the powered accessories, at least initially. This would go a long way to help in meeting the price objectives of the basic car.

The less-developed countries are having fewer problems in creating a basic car as they are upgrading from a scooter and a powered rickshaw, whereas the western countries need to not only downsize but to unload many luxury features that are prevalent on today's cars.

Many American customers view such a basic vehicle today with disdain, but their views or choice of vehicle will be modified by their diminishing personal wealth after a couple of years of recession conditions.

Apart from passenger cars there are other vehicles, i.e., light trucks, vans and highway trucks, all of which will have to go through a similar transformation to achieve compatibility with fuel economy objectives and a new fuel to replace oil. Of particular interest are the highway trucks which have played a vital role in the creation and maintenance of the Wondrous World we live in. Virtually everything we utilize in our daily lives involves large numbers of truck journeys both in its growing, manufacture and delivery which we depend on for our very existence.

There is general agreement among vehicle engineers that fuel-cells driving an electric motor and using a renewable fuel are the logical and desirable choice for powering future vehicles. Although hydrogen is the ideal fuel for powering a fuel cell, its manufacture from a renewable material has not been found possible to achieve efficiently or practically. The second best approach is to use a hydrogen carrier such as methanol for the fuel and extract the hydrogen from it with a reformer on the vehicle. A number of prototypes have been built using methanol as a tank fuel, but because of the academic and political support for pure hydrogen, they have been set aside. This approach avoids the issue of fuel handling and storage.

It is now necessary to recognize the practicality of choice and fully investigate, putting the effort behind methanol or similar types of bio-materials for hydrogen carriers as the tank fuel. This will also involve a parallel major agricultural program for growing trees and other biomass for deriving the fuel. These actions would break loose the logjam that now exists in this stagnated pond of technical conflict because of the hydrogen infatuation and start moving this vital program in a practical direction to resolve one of the world's major problems.

The reason for selecting automotive transportation fuel for special attention is because it is a problem that is already impacting the world crisis and could rapidly worsen. Resolving the issue of a renewable replacement for oil is also such a vital issue for maintaining our existence and coupled with its unique requirements, makes it the number one priority. If this transportation energy problem can be resolved, it will also go a long way in forming a basis for solving other major issues such as environment, population, sustainability and political conflicts.

The subject of an oil replacement has primarily being directed at passenger cars and other light vehicles, but there is also the subject of heavy highway trucks which are a major user of oil and have been a vital segment in the creation of the wondrous world we live in. Virtually everything we utilize in our daily lives has a network of trucking involved in its creation and delivery to the consumer. First, the raw basic materials transported to the source of production and then the final product may be involved in several more trucking legs before the item arrives at the point of sale or disposition. For example, peaches and other fruits and vegetables grown in California are shipped by truck all over the country and often abroad. Cars manufactured in Detroit are hauled by truck to dealerships in every corner of the country. Food, clothes, furniture and all other items are involved in this vast network of trucking or they would be sitting idle, deteriorating at that point of origin. The so-called highway truck is the vehicle that achieves this complicated marvel of distribution. It consists of a truck tractor which is the means of towing the trailer or trailers which are large storage boxes on wheels, usually 13 ft. high, 8 ft. wide and 40 ft. long. The space inside is open and uninterrupted except for a raised level at the front-end that is over the so called fifth wheel which is the point of connection to the tractor. The fifth wheel also provides the articulation between the tractor and trailer for maneuvering, and it is the means of separating the two units when parking or loading and unloading. Trailers are usually supported at their rear end by two axles with four or eight wheels.

Trailers are often fitted with air-conditioning and heating equipment to allow transportation of temperature sensitive cargo. They are usually towed one behind a tractor, but sometimes conditions are conducive to hooking up a second trailer particularly in the states which permit such rigs. There is also a network of trailer depots or marshaling yards so that these trailers can be dropped off or transferred to another tractor for continuing their progress to the final destination. The tractors are large, powerful machines usually with two front wheels for steering and two driving axles with four or eight wheels for propelling the vehicle. These are thirsty machines and often only achieve 1 or 2 MPG when used under loaded conditions. This explains why the heavy truck usage of crude oil fuel in the U.S. is some 3 million barrels per day.

The factors that determine mpg are the same as in the cars: weight, drag and aerodynamic shape. The weight is essentially inherent in the truck-trailer combination and cargo or payload. The drag is largely determined by the frontal area which is controlled by the 13 ft. high and 8 ft. wide trailers which are as aerodynamic as a brick. The only possible variation is in the form and streamlining of the tractor which is the most important factor for piercing the wind.

In the early 1960's, the planned 42,000 mile expansion of the interstate highway system was underway in recognition of the importance and efficiency of the transportation system. This encouraged the Ford Motor Company to explore the possibilities of how the only variable, the truck tractor, could be modified to improve the horribly inefficient MPG numbers and how to decrease the

time of delivery and improve the safety of drivers and rigs.

Figure 14 : Big-Red the Super-Highway Truck. (Courtesy Ford Motor Co)

The result of this exercise was the experimental superhighway truck known as "Big-Red." This vehicle was conceived around the objectives of making more efficient use of the new highway system and incorporating features for the comfort and convenience of the drivers thus providing conditions to help promote safety. It was designed with a tractor cab shape that totally blended in with the trailer cross section. It provided space and facilities for full living accommodations for two people. This included fully equipped driver and co-driver seating, a kitchen, toilet, shower and sleeping accommodation for an off duty driver. A photograph of the finish vehicle is shown in Figure 14. The vehicle could tow a single or double trailer rig in 120 feet long combination with the double trailer units. The tractor weight was 20,000 lbs., and the two trailers and dolly were 30,000 lbs. including a payload of 120,000 lbs. This all added up to a gross combination weight of 170,000 lbs.

The vehicle could cruise at 70 mph, and its fuel economy at this speed was 2.03 MPG compared to 1.7 MPG with the conventional rig. This was a fuel consumption improvement of 15%. Big-Red was used in the Ford transport system for shipping service department cargo from Detroit to Los Angeles on a regular basis. Big-Red's concept progressively influenced production vehicles starting with aerodynamic air deflectors fitted to the cab roofs to deflect the air over the flat ended trailers. Also, cabin interiors have since been improved, and some long-distance vehicles now have amenities for two people to travel and sleep in relative comfort. All of this has been accomplished with the old standard 13 ft. high, 8ft wide and 40 ft. long trailers. These have been kept high by the obsession to keep the trailer floor free from intrusion from the rear wheels. But now, however, there needs to be a drastic review in favor of a more fuel efficient new standard trailer unit which is lowered by 2- 2.5 ft. This new trailer would keep the same interior volume, but the rear wheels would intrude into the interior at the trailer's rear floor; however, there would still be room between the wheel arches to allow the loading machinery to operate from the rear end. This would lower the loading platform height from 4.5 ft. to 2-2.5 ft. creating the possibility of lowering the loading docks by an equivalent amount. The top of the tractor would be lowered to the same height as the trailer creating a substantial reduction in frontal area resulting in greater fuel economy and making the units less likely to roll over. It will also cut down on loading bay accidents. The improvement in fuel economy will be relative to the reduction in frontal area which is approximately 19% further improvement in MPG. Furthermore, the streamlined underbody of the trailer would be an added improvement in aerodynamic drag.

The frontal area and aerodynamic change also relates to a very important safety problem which is that of cars passing trucks or trucks passing cars in rainy weather. The danger is caused by the unbelievably bad aerodynamics of the present trailers and their over 4 feet of ground clearance under the floor. The turbulence stirs up water on the road so that the truck rig creates a cloud of water spray which virtually blinds car drivers. This is extremely dangerous, particularly at night. The improved aerodynamics created by lowering the vehicle to 2-21/2 feet and leaving only 2 feet of ground clearance and the resulting cleaned up bottom of the trailer

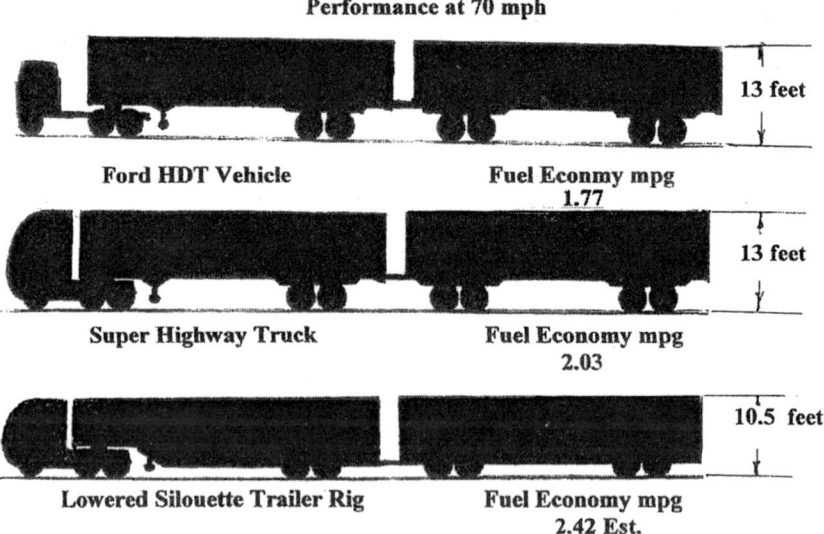

Figure 15: The original trailer rig compared to Fords Big-Red and the Proposed Lowered Silhouette Truck and Trailer.

would go a long way to improving this dangerous condition.

The resulting trailer would be similar to the units developed for beer and canned drink distribution and would create major improvements in fuel economy.

Figure 15 shows how the original trailer compared to Ford's Big-Red and the proposed new Lowered Silhouette trailer rig with an estimated 2.42 MPG. It should be noted that the overall fuel savings of 37% in miles per gallon from the original rig could result in U.S. trucks saving as much as 1 million barrels of crude oil per day. This would be a valuable contribution to the conservation program.

The issue of applying fuel cells to trucks will be similar to the problems encountered with the installation in cars, except the size of the units will be much larger. The type of unit might be different, but the fundamentals would be the same. The resulting trucks will be interesting running virtually silently except for the road and wind noise- a wonderful thought.

Aircraft are the most difficult machines in the whole automotive spectrum for which to find a renewable fuel to replace oil. Also nobody has made it a high a priority to develop a solution but ironically the space program which is only another form of Aeronautics, runs on liquid hydrogen and oxygen. Now new units are being developed to replace the shuttle that will use horizontal takeoff and landing. This will start to close the gap between space craft and supersonic planes.

As oil's demise progresses, this very important aircraft transportation segment will be the most affected. It could result in having to prioritize the usage of remaining oil for this purpose.

Shipping has already embarked on programs employing DEP (Diesel Electric Propulsion) which are comprised of diesel engines driving generators providing the electricity for the final drives that are electric motors housed in 360° rotatable pods. See

Figure 16. These pods allow for level propellers pointing in the desired direction of motion and only involve electric cable connections between primary and final power sources. This eliminates the rumbling of drive shafts and the inefficient angled propeller. It also provides unbelievable maneuverability and helps in the event of an engine failure by having the option of transferring the elec-

Mermaid azimuthing electric propulsion pods are a joint development by Alstom and Rolls Royce

tricity from one unit to another.

Figure 16 : 360 degree rotatable pods-Diesel-Electric shipping propulsion.

To convert such ships to fuel-cell primary sources would be a relatively simple design chain once cell units are available. One would only have to modify the design to delete the DEP unit and replace it with a fuel- cell. This arrangement would be used for inshore activities with open ocean transportation most likely reverting to the original medium of wind. There are now experimental ships being tested and developed which take the form of the old original square rigger sailing boat and disposes of its negatives by using rotating rigging-less masts. If this development is successful, the transatlantic vessels of the future could use wind exclusively, except for close inshore navigation and to access rivers and harbors, etc. A romantically named vessel called the *Maltese Falcon* is a test vehicle of this form of development and has already been successfully sailing in the Mediterranean for several years. See Figure 17.

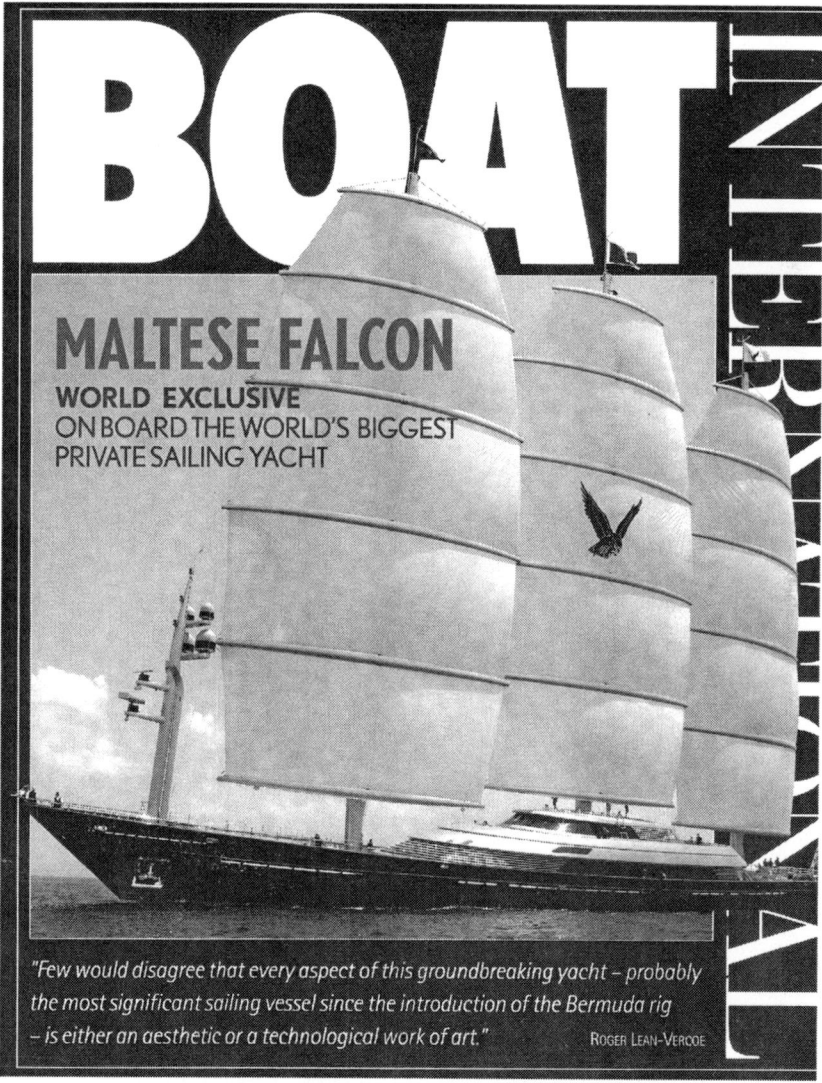

Figure 17: Maltese Falcon sailing vessel.

Chapter 12

AGRICULTURE

Returning once more to the beginning of the nineteenth century, it was a time when the world was still based on an agricultural economy, but drastic changes were underway. From the beginning of human civilization to that time, many people worked on the land and understood the nature of soil, the seasons, plants and animals. These factors were the supporters of life by providing the food needed for their existence and sustainability. Today in the western world, there are comparatively few farmers and only a few percent of the population work on, or understand, the land.

The change started to come about with the Industrial Revolution in the second half of the eighteenth century which brought with it the mechanization of all commercial activities including farming. This freed up huge numbers of the population who moved to the cities to work in the factories. Farming then progressed from the old mixed farming format to the crop specialization or "mono-cropping" which was made possible not only by mechanization but also transportation. Crops were then able to be grown in abundance, very often at great distances from their final market instead of all the produce being grown locally in small mixed lots. This not only required the produce to be distributed nationally but in many cases internationally or even globally. This phase was followed by increased volume achieved by chemical usage including fertilization and pesticides to prevent loss to insects and disease. Many of these chemicals were fossil-based materials, i.e., phosphates, which have to be mined thereby increasing the land degradation problem. The final item in this series of development is genetically modified products to aid in increasing quality and volume in this mass production process. The whole subject of food production and distribution has been exacerbated by not only oil fuel for farming and transportation but also refrigeration and the advent of supermarkets replacing main street stores.

The big shift from mixed farming to intensive mono-cropping started after WW II and was encouraged and even subsidized by governments who wanted increased food production. The whole change took an extensive investment of money and technology, and this consequently pushed out the small farmers, and the world's food industry is now in the hands of twenty or so mega companies whose main objective is naturally to generate profit. However, the whole agricultural situation is now starting to change. It is evident that in every major problem the world faces, renewable recyclable crops are likely to be a large part of the solution. These problems start with the population explosion that will require increased food production to feed them, ending with a resolution of the energy and environment issues. This requires the progressive cessation of mining and the reduction of burning oil and coal which should be replaced with renewable materials which are highly likely to be derived from recyclable crops to provide continuing sustainability.

To start mono-cropping or mass farming, a corporation must first acquire large areas of contiguous farm acreage. It is then necessary to clear all trees, hedgerows and obstacles to allow for easy access and operation of machinery. To provide for efficient watering it is then necessary to flatten and level the massive fields to within a fraction of an inch to make flood irrigation possible. This involves moving thousands of cubic yards of soil with large driverless earth moving equipment controlled by lasers, GPS and radio. The soil is then prepared physically and chemically prior to seeding the vast mono-crop that can be planted and maintained by machine with a minimum of difficulty. The harvesting is also highly mechanized as are the selection and packaging processes to provide a perfect looking product. Then the distribution, nation-wide or internationally, is accomplished by a vast network of refrigerated trailer trucks, and, if appropriate, by ships. Selecting and preparing the perfect looking produce generates a very high percentage of waste from the raw product and from the associated packing and wrapping materials, but the whole system provides the consumer with eye pleasing fruits and vegetables very often year round and achieves for the corporations the objectives of making a profit.

Unfortunately, the agriculture mono-cropping system described is not self- sustaining and brings with it a number of unacceptable negatives. The total clearing of land and its chemical preparation kills off the natural structure of animals and insects which are a basic part of nature's natural cycle of events to grow and protect vegetation. These vary from the earthworms to insect chains to natural soil nutrients and even the presence of birds because of their loss of habitat. The agricultural chemicals, many of which are fossil based or non-renewable, can also contaminate the end products themselves as well as the vital water supply. Constantly using chemicals without plowing in crop waste can cause a vicious cycle of events that without crop and land use cycling, can leave the product nutritionally questionable. This is because the produce can contain portions of the chemicals used in the growing process.

The high use of oil energy is of utmost importance to the present mono-crop farming system. It is used in every phase of land preparation, growing, processing and delivery of the produce where engine driven machinery is used. The oil supply issue is likely to eventually result in the need for returning to the use of the old methods of mixed farming known as "Natures Way" to maintain sustainability. These old natural methods of growing crops are often not as fast or profitable as the highly mechanized based production used to day. However, they can produce some wonderful results as illustrated by the wine making episode in France at the end of WW II.

As the German army commenced its retreat, the French people immediately started activities to reopen the vineyards and make wine again. Conditions were far from ideal as most of the young men were still absent. They had been drafted to German factories, and the only males remaining were very young or very old. The principal workers were, therefore, the women who had been left to run the farms and vineyards. As these ladies planned the growing and harvesting of the 1945 vintage, they were hampered by many factors. Not only were most of the men away, they were lacking many of the wine making ingredients. These included sulphur, fertilizer and other chemicals, and in addition, there was no sugar, and because of a bottle shortage, the wine had to remain in the casks longer which gave it more character. One thing that was going for them was the weather which was ideal and produced fat, juicy grapes to work with. The result was a small harvest, but the quality was exceptional. Critics gave it six stars out of five and the 1945 vintage became, and still is, regarded as the wine of the century.

Cuba has become an interesting representation of this modern organic or sustainable type of farming. Cuba was an industrialized based farming country, using agrochemicals that were highly dependent on Russia for their supply until 1989 when the Soviet Union collapsed. This forced Cuba into being self-supporting and revert to mixed farming which they achieved by scientifically identifying the natural organisms of biofertilizers and biopesticides and then mass producing them synthetically to replace the unavailable chemicals. This natural process progressed, and today Cuba is the world leader and best example of how it is possible to revert from industrialized chemical based mass farming to nature's sustainable "Natures Way" in a relatively short period of time.

When the degradation from mining chemicals is finally realized and reacted to and the oil energy availability is reduced, there will be economic and supply issues which will generate pressures to return to a locally mixed farming with a sustainable base for food products. An exception for the continued use of mono-cropping may be "energy crop farming" that is likely to involve plantings that are more suitable to ploughing back crop waste and not using excessive chemicals.

Another reason for returning to mixed farming is a concern that many illnesses and diseases, including obesity, may be the result of chemically contaminated products. There is also an open issue on assessing the true nutrient content of products and not just considering volume or quantity.

A parallel to agricultural farming is dairy or live stock farming which has gone through radical changes and is now due for re-examination.

Before entering a discussion of the issues involving livestock, it is worth a brief review on man's attitude towards animals. Going back into history, man's first reaction to animals was one of defense for his survival. As time went on killing them became a source for supplying humans with digestible nutrients and led to hunting and fishing activities not for defense but for food and other by-products such as fur. Over many thousands of years man's attitude to animals has changed radically even though killing certain species for food has continued. On the other hand, man has developed a respect and even love for animals and even accepts some, such as cats and dogs, to share his habitat with him. There has also been a progressive feeling of concern for these creatures which has generated protection measures for them. This has taken many forms, i.e., hunting and shooting restrictions, endanged species protection and humane laws for their habitation and killing. More recently, changes of circuses from animal performances to human ones, the banning of fox hunting in England, the protesting of wearing fur coats and increased vegetarianism for religious and health based reasons have occurred. All these actions have helped lessen the suffering of animals, although there is still a large segment of inhuman practices relating to keeping and killing farm animals.

The general public reacts with disgust as it learns more about the cruel and inhumane methods used in livestock farming. Chickens are kept in batteries that restrict the bird's movement, and they are fed on one side of the cage, and the eggs are collected in racks on the other. Their droppings fall through the cage bottom, and when the chickens egg laying days are over, the birds are killed for their meat. Pigs are also kept in unbelievably restricted and filthy conditions. Cows are kept in a constant state of pregnancy and develop huge udders, the weight of which cripples the animal beyond being able to stand up. And killing young animals for veal is a well known factor.

The cruel and filthy conditions in which all these animals are kept breeds disease and necessitates the excessive use of antibiotics in their feed. This alarms the medical profession because the end product carries portions of the drugs to the consumer which can result in developing drug resistance to diseases.

The percentage of time that animals spend feeding in natural pastures has decreased while the percentage of chemical based animal feed is increasing. The main aim is to speed-up growth of the animals to make them bigger quicker and provide greater profit. Again, the chemical content in feed can be reflected in the end product with questionable results including nutrient levels.

The long distance shipping of animals has also increased dramatically in recent years with the creatures suffering still further appalling conditions. Historians will look back at this period with dismay.

Another influencing issue is the fact that rearing animals takes considerably more land and feed then growing vegetation of an equivalent nutrient value. This quickly brings up the subject of land usage which is the key to any long term plan for a sustainable future in agriculture.

It is argued by many that most arable land is already in use, and there is only room for limited expansion because of factors such as water. Yet, one can fly over America and any country in the world and look down on vast areas of vacant land. This is true, if to a lesser degree, in the highly populated countries of Europe. Then there are the vast desert areas of the world where there is almost no land use and very few people. The discrepancy in opinions on land use expansion is largely due to the definition of arable land and for what it is likely to be used. The pessimists on availability are correct if the land under review is expected to be rich, virgin soil with rivers and streams running across it.

Unfortunately, many areas are not like this and have inbuilt problems that prevent them from being used for cultivating crops. The "Badlands" of South Dakota is an example of this because their soil depth is very limited, and the under strata is rock that is very close to the surface. Even these lands, however, are sometimes suitable for grazing cattle. Then there are the vast open desserts which, in their present condition, have poor soil and are mostly sand. These are often areas which originally supported vegetation and will take a great deal of effort to reclaim.

Probably the best known large desert area of the world is the Sahara which geological historians tell us was once covered with forest and vegetation and supported a moderate climate due to the interaction of the vegetation with the weather. Driving across the Sahara, one starts to appreciate its size. One can drive for days without seeing any appreciable sign of habitation. By taking a world globe and outlining on tracing paper the mainland of the United States and then laying it over the Sahara desert, one would notice that the U.S. outline drops into the space without touching the sides. Another factor that is amazing to witness is that the few people that live there usually have no means of transport except walking or riding a camel, have no communication, i.e., telephone, TV, newspapers, etc., have never seen a running faucet and don't know the meaning of a toilet, toilet paper or bathing; very often their information is only what was passed on to them by their family who were also illiterate and primitive.

An example of their unfortunate lack of knowledge is encountered when traveling through the countries lining the Sahara's southern border. This is an area where there are still some trees and vegetation, and some primitive low level farming is taking place with only humans and animals as a source for power. Traversing these areas in the month of January one is often conscious of the smell of burning material and sometimes the presence of smoke.

This is because they still use the ancient slash and burn method of clearing land for next year's crops which causes a progressive loss of arable land to the desert. From time to time one encounters smoke and can even hear the crackling of the burning wood.

A little education and support would go a long way in halting this primitive process and perhaps make a start at reclaiming the desert. There was some hope when these countries were part of the French Empire, but their so called independence after WW II lost them this source of education. It also brought low level government with questionable ethics.

An opposite extreme of land use utilization also occurred after WW II when the British handed Palestine back to the Jews and Arabs. In this case, the Jewish individuals returning to their homeland were largely educated and dedicated to creating a better life, and coincidently, much of the time they were dealing with dried arid land similar to many of the African countries.

The Jewish people living in the western world are not known for their prowess as gardeners. It was therefore interesting in 1948 when the Jewish government established the requirement for those returning to Palestine to serve on the land for six months before settling. This applied to all people including doctors, lawyers, architects, etc. It was a most sensible way of getting the population to know the land and understand its importance to providing a sustaining existence and for their own future and well being.

The Jewish settlers developed an interesting way of taking arid desert and converting it to arable land. They made tiny flower pots from biodegradable cardboard, filled them with soil and planted tree seeds in them. These plants were initially kept in crude greenhouses and given a few drops of water each day. When they became a few inches tall, the whole pot was planted out in the open desert and they continued to patiently give them a few drops of water each day. As the trees grew, their roots pushed out through the paper pots and into the secondary sandy soil. Through constant nurturing, the trees grow, and in time weeds grew around them then they added a few goats which provided the fertilizer and completed nature's natural cycle of events. Apparently, the action of the roots growing in the sand progressively changed it to arable soil. The result of this exercise produced vegetated meadows and fertile land for orchards and farming.

It was a good example of how educated dedicated people can change the definition of what is arable and what is not. This drastically changes the estimation of how much land is available if needed, and as a side issue, the basic process of reclaiming land would restart land commercialization. This in turn could provide employment for many of the destitute people in these desolate areas.

Taking all factors into consideration, it is highly likely that in a few generations there will be more of a trend towards vegetarianism as crops takes less land area than pasture.

Restoring and reclaiming land is likely to be a major ongoing task to support the infrastructure for the development of renewable fuels and the increased need for sustenance crops to feed the increasing population. Doing this in arid desserts while seeking to find the best energy fuels is likely to be achieved by the use of trees. In general, they are more adaptable to poor soil and require less water than ground crops. They also give shade, provide oxygen generating factors and favorably modify climate and weather patterns which in turn could help to generate rain.

Returning arid land to agricultural use is most probably the most important factor in creating a sustainable future for the world and influencing the weather cycle with the important factor of rain and storms.

It is also interesting to note that going through the factors involved with returning to an agricultural base, demonstrates the

AGRICULTURE

importance of reviewing all major problems simultaneously in order to establish common denominator solutions. Returning land for farming use can provide the renewable sources for energy crops to be grown. This not only helps the energy issue but also provides a source of employment for the illiterate unemployed. This is the key to better living in the less developed countries where basic education is necessary for controlling the birth rate which in turn helps to solve the population issue. Returning to a farming base also helps to replace mining by returning to "Nature's Way" which in turn helps to solve major environmental problems.

To replant the face of the world might sound like a tremendous job. It is, but its straightforward, old-fashioned gardening on a grand scale. It just takes an organized long term plan to include the clearing, digging and irrigation, and it takes a great deal of patience as it will take several generations to accomplish, but it is possible. For instance, if the American army and other world military powers were charged with participating in the task, it would start making progress immediately. Also, having all the military equipment replaced with farming equipment would make armies welcome, instead of hated, in any country they visited.

Not only will returning to an agricultural economy bring improvements in the three major problem areas of population, energy and environment, but it will also make the world a much cleaner, peaceful and better place to live and help to provide the world with essential sustainability and peace.

We have to realize that the subject of agriculture cannot be looked at as being secondary importance or status or left to massive corporations to exploit, as they see fit, for corporate greed. It is the key to the world's sustainability.

Chapter 13

EDUCATION

Education is the most formidable of all human capabilities which come to us in many ways. It starts in the form of copying and repetition which is usually passed to an infant by the family. This process continues into exercising all five senses together with conversation for several years until the child can communicate its wishes and demands. Then in association with others, it starts to assimilate a variety of capabilities until the formal learning of the three R's commences. These subjects are necessary as the basics for all future learning together with the mental factors of logical processing. Even though the internet is a new forum for storing and transferring knowledge, the three R's of reading, writing and arithmetic are still the necessary basics of learning that the individual normally starts to learn in his early years from the family at home. Unfortunately, a sad by-product of the highly developed world we live in is its detrimental effect on the family unit.

In general, 200 years ago people didn't travel far from home. It was common for people to be born, raised, married, raise a family and eventually retire and be buried in the same town or area. This type of living produced a strong family unit with the younger persons aiding their relatives in time of trouble and old age and the adults participating in the children's educational lessons. As communications and transportation developed, families often progressively split up. The children sometimes left home for education purposes or seeking employment. As a result they often married persons from faraway places, and when their parents retired, they also frequently migrated to different areas in warmer climates. This whole process has weakened or destroyed the family unit with its day to day contact of family members. It has also forced the development of governmental as well as private support systems such as care centers and retirement homes with limited availability and are a poor substitute for the family circle.

Another factor leading to the deterioration of the family circle is the subject of divorce. The rate of divorce has escalated rapidly in recent years with a further resulting breakup of the family unit. There are obviously many reasons for this but some can certainly be attributed to the modern way of living. More leisure time, easier communications, more marriages with both partners working and a freer workplace and social behavior all have an effect. It is inevitable that scientific development and invention that have helped create this world would also have undesirable by-products which have resulted in a lack of parents helping in the educational process of their children and particularly in becoming involved with the issue of parental control.

Centers of learning date back for thousands of years, but general public schools such as we have today are a comparatively modern institution. They are attributed to Charlemagne in the

8th century A.D. when he recognized the need for educating the general public. To make this possible, he needed buildings and teachers and the Roman Catholic Church and monks provided the answer. Thus, parochial schools were born, and formal general learning began.

Educational systems have changed considerably in the last 200 years. They have advanced dramatically from the one room schools which often covered the whole range of ages from five to college level. This was achieved with a single teacher teaching all levels and all subjects. The only facilities were a pot-bellied stove for heating and an outhouse for sanitation. Today, there are a wide range of schools starting with kindergarten. Then follows a variety of levels through grade school and progresses through middle school to high school. Each level has several teachers for teaching different subjects and generally covers a limited age range. The subjects included not only the called for 3 R's but many of the arts and sciences and physical training or sports as well. In the western world the facilities involved are usually large, well-lit classrooms, specially equipped laboratories and gymnasiums, etc. Most are well heated and sometimes even air-conditioned and have a full range of modern facilities. In addition, some have basketball arenas, playing fields, pools and tennis courts which are not only used during the day but also for after school activities.

The grade school system usually finishes at about ten years old and is followed by middle and high school which take the students to eighteen years old. It is sometimes augmented by prep schools for helping to prepare the students for college or university educations. These higher education systems also include various technical schools and junior colleges which sometimes issue 2-year degrees or certificates of capability. Then there are the main university systems which not only provide for 4 year degrees but also post graduate work covering both general and specialized subjects as well as research.

This vast structure of educational facilities has been built up to provide the ongoing maintenance and development of our way of life. It is also the critical element in exploring the future and continuing to create improvements. These institutions, however, are not without their problems.

All compulsory education systems from kindergarten through high school are today plagued by an unruly minority which has little desire for learning and high desire to cause trouble. They are largely a by-product of the new wondrous world's easier, relaxed, freer style of living with its weakened family unit factor. This minor percentage of students has a major influence on the whole teaching system. In addition, teaching staff are limited in using old established methods of disciplinary control, and new methods have not yet been developed. As a result, it is a breeding ground for a huge variety of crimes that range from drugs, stealing, gun possession, vandalism, sex and even murder. It is a little worrying to think of these undesirables entering the adult world with all its opportunities for good and bad.

It is therefore necessary to look at the total system of teaching methods to try and infuse possible correcting factors. It has been suggested that going back to separate male and female facilities, up to the end of high school, would alleviate many of the problems. This is most probably true, but it does necessitate doubling-up of facilities. Another possible alternative is to change the system by differently dividing up job functions and responsibilities by making further use of modern electronic systems.

In most cases today, the teacher is expected not only be capable of teaching by giving the lesson or lecture, but also administering the class logistics and keeping disciplinary control. Their only retaliation to a rebellious student is usually a threat to send the offending student to the principal's office. Conveying the course of the events clearly to the principles can sometimes be difficult.

The tools already available in many classrooms have turned them into electronic lecture halls. Some class rooms are already fitted with projectors and screens together with sound equipment. Installing a surveillance camera with recording and online viewing capability is an easy addition. The subjects to be taught can be recorded by a highly capable lecturer who is likely to also have the capability to better hold student attention. All illustrations would be built into the film or slides which would save the time of the teacher drawing them on a board. The class teacher would be present and available to answer questions, apply class discipline, provide logistical support and control and mark homework. Knowing they are being viewed by camera would, hopefully, automatically be a deterrent to the trouble makers while being taught by the best possible teachers. Making this "Big Brother" approach possible would necessitate clearing all legal factors which appears to be the major limiting factor at the moment.

To expect young teachers, newly out of college, to be able to prepare a course, write the lessons and present them while making illustrations on the board and trying to keep control of unruly students is a little ambitious. The electronic system would be a double edged sword because it would also provide a check on the teacher's capabilities in addition to providing a record of events. The electronic world is here, and making even fuller use of it could provide an assured level of excellent teaching and student control if only the lawyers and teacher unions can be brought into agreement.

To visit a well-equipped modern American classroom is impressive. In addition to the electronic blackboard, there are sometimes televisions, reproduction equipment for copying and printing and the all important "Computer at every desk." The one room school is something out of ancient history.

The more developed countries have channels of learning from preschool to universities and beyond, but this is not universal. The less developed countries often have minimal level of facilities or sometimes none at all. A world globalization objective has to be providing a learning opportunity for everyone. It is the only way to facilitate birth control and prepare persons for meaningful occupational involvement in order to be able to help themselves. Again, religious systems provide an opportunity, but their prevailing teachings are not always conducive to solving the problem. For example, the previously mentioned, unrealistic "sexual abstinence" approach to birth control is totally against natural instincts. But, if the religious sects would update and globalize their teachings, they would again be an obvious opportunity for the basis for expanding the school system in the undeveloped countries as were Charlemagne's abbeys and monks in the 8th century.

Much of the undeveloped or developing world has a male dominated culture which often excludes educating the female gender. This is an issue that the religious institutions could help to resolve. Also, providing the males with full-time occupational activities would lead to providing schools and a learning opportunity for both genders to generate a basis for establishing their civil rights and liberties.

Chapter 14

GOVERNMENTAL

Management: Through the centuries there have been many systems and types of government. These initially ranged from tribal chiefs to kingdoms to a group type of control, or management. Some were elected, others appointed, and in the case of royalty, mostly inherited. A reason for the selection of a particular type of political system was sometimes historic evolution or the result of a takeover. The takeover was sometimes the result of a coup, aggression or an uprising which left the military chief in charge or some other politician or person he appointed or supported. Another category of people management is based on religion; this is where the spiritual leaders take charge of all the civil systems. In other words, combining Church and State. The extent of any governmental administration can be local, regional, countrywide or even over several countries.

The more developed western countries have mostly settled down to a democratic form of control which is usually elected, and its operation is based on some or all of the following factors:

- Freely elected by majority vote.
- One man one vote.
- Freedom of speech.
- No prejudice of sex, color or creed.
- Makes and approves decisions by majority vote.
- More than one party.
- Separation of church and state.
- A central currency.
- A principle language.
- Protects human rights.
- One set of laws.
- Operating with a free market system
- Usually guided by a mandate or constitution.

Some countries in the world have changed, or are changing, from one form of government to another. Normally, this is a change from a dictatorship to a democracy or a free market system. This can be a speedy action resulting from an uprising or revolution to a well-planned and controlled program applied over a period of time. Russia is an example of the former, and China is most probably the best representation of the latter.

The modern world is a mixture of all forms, levels and types of government which is proving to make it difficult to attain joint resolution of global issues. The whole situation is both hindered and helped by the electronic age where communication is virtually instantaneous. Consequently, there are few secret actions anymore, and any move is quickly known and reacted to, and usually the debate becomes open for all to see.

The current organizing body on a world wide basis is the United Nations (U.N.) which was preceded by the League of Nations which started operating in 1920. The League of Nations was dissolved with the advent of WWII, and the U.N. began after the war. Although a great deal of time and money has been spent on the U.N, it's effectiveness and integrity is still questionable even though it has developed extensive data gathering capability; its size and political structure make it a cumbersome, slow moving entity with only limited delegated authority.

All political systems are devised and run by humans and are subject to man's strengths and weaknesses. Trying to be authoritarian and democratic at the same time is a contradiction in terms, but it may be possible to take advantage of both these systems in the course of time. The dictatorship has the obvious problem that it's difficult to impose controls to assure the whims and fancies of the ruler do not get out of control. The democracy has a problem that there are so many checks and balances in its control system, it is difficult to get anything done.

It is interesting to note that much of the world has developed totally different approaches for running its political and business systems. In contrast to the highly democratized political approach, business has developed a totally contrary authoritarian model. It is one in which the human capabilities are exploited for the corporate good by appropriate rewards ranging from personal achievement, pride of authorship and satisfaction to financial incentives.

The typical business structure of a company producing a competitive product is the Board of Directors, representing the stockholders. They establish the policy and appoint a president, or Chief Operating Officer, who is responsible for executing their programs and projects. The president is delegated the authority and budget together with the freedom of decision making to bring the program to a successful conclusion. The president is expected to consider the inputs of his subordinates, but the final decision is his to make. In selecting the president, the BOD judgmentally makes sure that he or she has the education, experience and personality to meet the corporate objectives. For all intents and purposes, the president is an appointed dictator, although he is required to operate by an acceptable code of ethics. Checks and balances are accomplished by progressive evaluation and reporting. The final evaluation of the President is the corporation's success in the marketplace and the bottom line of the balance sheet. This approach brings out the human traits of working hard with the freedom of decision making and the rewards being achievement, satisfaction and financial success.

The main sequence of events that enables the company to operate is as follows:

- Firstly, the shareholders have to have money to acquire equity of ownership.

- Secondly, the Board of Directors (BOD) must have a range of talents, both educationally and empirically, to be able to contribute to forming company policy. Also having good management judgment on choosing an appropriate president, together with providing sound financial guidance is essential.

- Thirdly, the president has to have appropriate education and work experience to satisfy the BOD's selection.

This is in contrast to the political system where the public is not required to have any vested interest to vote other than being a citizen in good standing. The political party's grass roots members, who are in general the equivalents of the BOD, are not required to have any formal education level, previous experience or equity, and, likewise, the presidential candidate has only to have the ability to convince the voting public by one means or another. But his or her education and experience level is not a major criterion. In the case of the U.S. President, he does have to be born an American citizen and be at least 35 years old.

In addition to this lack of requirements for politicians is the over cumbersome factor that every move has to be by a majority vote of the legislature. Also, the check and balance factors of having an opposition party operating continuously absolutely destroys the efficiency of having a unified team with all members trying to contribute and make progress in the same direction. If businesses were run like governments with majority votes being prevalent at every stage, they would be totally uncompetitive. In many ways it seems as though government is one of the last strongholds of inefficient amateurism.

An interesting U.S. constitutional issue is the separation of Church and State. It is a factor which arises frequently with such issues as birth control, same sex marriage, abortion, sex education, the death penalty, etc. Politicians' opinions are often swayed by the voting weight of religious groups, and it is extremely difficult to keep religion as a separate entity. Also, the country as a whole is labeled as Christian although many religions are present, and a large portion of the population only has religious involvement by birth denomination. This is in contrast to some other political systems which have a formal linking between religion and government.

There is an obvious need for individuals to have a faith which gives them spiritual association with God. This association is referred to in the U.S. Constitution with the words "In God we Trust." The issue has become further clouded by the Evolution-Creation debate. Most scientists agree that although they have the evidence to support the evolution of the world, there is still the presence of an almighty being. They have pretty well traced the evolution from a slug-like creature crawling out of the water and eventually evolving into humans. But, there are still huge open issues of who created the slug, guided the course of development and gave humans a brain and a soul. This mysterious unknown is usually designated God, who is worshipped and communicated with through prayer.

A few of the religious fraternities use the Old Testament of the Bible for their religions basis and some take such items as the seven days of creation literally. What they don't acknowledge is the fact that these scriptures were usually written by a scribe and were the deliberations of the wise men of the time after they had communed with God. They were the philosophers of the day, several thousands of years ago, who answered the people's questions, and it was a time when language was prevalent but very few could read or write.

The issues between the Evolutionists and Creationists, therefore, become sensitive when the religious groups lobby for Creationism to be taught in schools in place of science. This is particularly dangerous at a time when high levels of scientific capability are needed to solve such issues as renewable replacements for fossil materials and the development of a whole new range of transportation vehicles. Humans need spiritual involvement which is a very important part of government management, but it has to be kept in prospective.

The whole issue is one which, again, illustrates the need for the various religions to interrelate and debate. In the process the common denominator factors between religions should emerge.

The major religions were mainly generated during the last 3,000 years which was way before the extent of the world was even known. The subject of faith and spiritual needs has evolved to become a major factor in world events. It will, therefore, be important to include consideration of the spiritual factors of religion in any updated or new governmental management system even though it may take many decades to accomplish.

It has often been said that the present form of western democracy may not be the perfect governmental system, but it is the best that has been found so far. But the desire for equality and checks and balances has progressively generated complexities which impair its efficiency of operations and makes it overly bureaucratic and cumbersome. Forward thinking, planning and experimentation over a period time will be necessary to evolve a more efficient system. Ironically, despite the recently demonstrated shortcomings of the present democratic system, it is touted to the less developed countries as the only way to go. These impositions on other political systems which often have different cultural associations and backgrounds are regarded as western interference and become the cause of many of the world's conflicts that are prevalent or may happen in the future. The problems caused by forcing political systems on others are sometimes also accompanied by religious pressure which aggravates the situations still further.

International-Governmental law started to become an issue in the 15th century as the entire world became apparent, and boundaries needed definition. Most of the early legislation developments on an international level were between Western European states. As these western powers expanded their colonial empires, they imposed their own laws on a world wide basis to make conquest easier and more convenient to run.

These international laws became more meaningful after WWI when a greater number of countries became involved in attempting and planning a more sustainable peace. Woodrow Wilson was, apparently, the principal instigator of what became the League of Nations that included over 40 nations but, ominously, not the U.S. The league established a covenant which fell apart with the advent of WWII when the league was not willing, or able, to control the expansionist plans of Germany, Japan and Italy.

The United Nations was instituted after WWII and drew up a charter with the same basic objectives as the League of Nations. Although the U.N. charter is the primary document of international law, the U.N. does not have the power or freedom to operate independently. The founding powers of the U.N, being the victors of WWII, which included the U.S. and U.S.S.R, China, France and the UK, allocated themselves permanent seats on the Security Council with full veto power over decisions relating to war and peace. This inherent impediment in the international rule system leaves the developing countries with inequality of power even though they may be sizable entities. The arrangement ensures that the group of five maintains control and are able to make sure their interests are best served regardless of the impact on less developed countries. It is reported that the U.N. now has 191 states in its membership and has grown into a huge entity with predominant involvements in dealing with war, peace and human rights. The U.N.'s secondary activities center on management of global activities including environmental factors. It has processed over 50,000 international treaties and agreements, administered the international court of justice, provided widespread peacekeeping forces, has a vast data gathering facility and should be truly the global management center. Unfortunately, its leadership is usually chosen to be the least offensive, but not necessarily the most capable.

It is an appropriate time to review the U.N. organization to make sure it is in keeping with the current needs and times. It would seem logical to separate its long term planning side, with its vast data gathering capabilities into a separate entity for studying the future and coming up with proposed solutions to world issues. Their mandate would be to gather facts and assess the long-term probability based on best scientific evidence and without the influence of short term profit or politics. Its sphere of operations could include relatively short-term of, perhaps, up to a hundred years and ongoing involvements of hundreds of years and long-term which would be beyond a thousand years. Their overall objective would be to be able to anticipate and plan for returning to a continuing and sustaining existence for the future. It would need an internationally selected authority to write its mandate and be operationally free of the main U.N. assembly and to make reports and recommendations on a continuing and open ended time basis.

It has been said that, "All rules are useless unless they are enforceable," which brings up the issue of military force. It is hard to comprehend that at this time in history, with so much advancement and refining of human ways of living, that physical wars still exist. This is particularly mystifying when one realizes that weapons have been developed to a capability level of inflicting complete annihilation. This situation then ignites the argument of who has a right to own such a capability which in turn generates the nonsensical discussion on limited warfare. Present international law states that "war is permissible only to repel an armed attack." But this has been interpreted to be "in self- defense and has been further distorted to be in anticipation of imminent threat of attack."

With such issues as a severe oil crisis looming on the horizon, one hopes that some disillusioned politician won't push the "go button" for war because the United States' way of life is being threatened. Armies run on oil, and it would be ironic to have the world's most powerful war machines fighting those with all the oil. It is only hoped that common sense will prevail, and that with time armed forces as such will be progressively replaced with peacekeeping or policing personnel.

There are a variety of related subjects of a less serious nature that are progressively being resolved or processed by the U.N. They include the standardization of weights and measures which is primarily between the English and metric systems. The metric system has the logical relationship of the factors involved and has been adopted by the scientific community and most countries, with the notable exception of the U.S. During the 1960's and 1970's, there was a program launched to change the U.S. to a metric based system. This was well underway when the president was persuaded to abort the program because of the inconvenience to the public and detraction from expanding the economy. Fortunately, many industries, such as the vehicle manufacturers, continued and virtually completed the change. The aircraft industry did not, nor did any of the public related actions of road signs, maps, food packaging and parceling, etc.

It is interesting to note that at about the same period, England adopted the Metric system for all aspects of its commercial and civil life. It was even more difficult for them because they not only had to convert weights and measures but also their whole money system which was unbelievably complex. It included 12 pennies to a shilling, 20 shillings to a pound, 21 shillings to a guinea and a range of coinage including a farthing, which is a quarter of a penny, a half penny, the penny, a three penny piece, a six Penney piece, the shilling, a two shilling piece, called a florin, and a two and a half shilling piece called a half-crown. The period of change to the ten based metric system was straight forward and a great simplification, but the logistics of its transition were complex. They used duel weights and measures for a period until metric progressively became second nature. The change was consolidated by the new generation who only had to learn metric. The exercise was accomplished successfully, and history will hardly notice the inconvenience or disruption.

Although America's money system is already in metric, the rest of its activities still need to be converted. But now it will be more difficult than doing it in the 1970's, and the longer it's delayed, the more difficult it will become. It is necessary to change not only to align with the rest of the world but all the sciences and most engineering systems are already using metric. Teaching new generations two systems is an unnecessary and confusing burden on the school system. In the U.S. the public only learns the English system in grade school and has to learn the metric system if their business experience dictates.

Another issue that eventually needs rectifying is that half the world drives on the right hand side of the road and the other half on the left. History relates many factors for these differences. Which horse, of the pair, on which the driver chooses to sit, makes it convenient to carry his whip in his right hand? Or, on which side the single horse rider carries his sword relative to oncoming, possibly unfriendly traffic. The issue becomes a safety factor in neighboring countries where drivers cross borders regularly because this involves a visiting driver sitting on the curbside with limited views of traffic with resulting safety issue. The change, when it occurs, will involve considerable planning and control.

There is an amusing story about the English who apparently considered the change from left hand side to right hand side driving. But being of a conservative nature they thought it would be appropriate to make the change gradually, starting with heavy trucks first.

Unifying of global rules and regulations becomes more imperative with sea and air traffic. Both of these activities are also monitored through the U.N. with its various departments: International Maritime Organization (IMO) and the International Civil Aviation Organization (ICAO).

Standardizing shipping laws and rules dates back to 1789 and international meetings held in 1889. The issues covered safety, navigation, charting, rules of the road, insurance and a myriad of nautical subjects including the fact that speed and distance are measured in knots and nautical miles. Through the years many issues have found agreement but there are still differences, particularly with buoys and markers and again the right side-left side issue. The shape and color and light designations are also still points to be unified.

The U.N. has little jurisdiction over the members of the I. M. O. as each country has its own choice of rules and enforcement laws. It is therefore incumbent on any prudent captain to become familiar with the local rules and charts before venturing into foreign waters.

The aviation fraternity, although much younger, is much better organized and unified in its acceptance of rules and regulations. These include airspace traffic rules, using the metric system designation of terms for speed distance and height and many other procedural factors together with English as the communication language. All this adds up to making flying safer, and in general, the aviation world operates according to the rules. Exceptions exist such as the occasional obstinate national language freak who refuses to use English to communicate.

Both the maritime and aeronautical fraternities have benefited greatly from the advancements in electronic development. Notable amongst these is the communications satellite system which, among other things, has spawned the Geographical Positioning System (GPS). This has revolutionized navigation factors and made communications easier and virtually instantaneous. Detection and surveillance systems have also improved immeasurably and, combined with improvements in weather forecasting, have all added up to safer travel.

As globalization activities increase, time will progressively help to resolve open issues and any new problems that might arise.

Governmental laws and management systems need to encompass all aspects of world trade in order to provide the means for countries to evolve and develop. This issue has caused considerable debate between free trade advocates and the protectionists. Much of the concern stems from job exportation which is a natural by-product of open markets. But no country is self supporting enough, with all the materials and services, to develop independently in this modern world. It is very necessary to create an exchange of goods and services to maintain and continue to improve the standard of living. An example of this is the subject of oil which has become an essential part of the world's and America's way of life. At this point in time, it is necessary for the U.S. to import 70% of the oil it uses. This is partially offset by exporting such items as grains, of which the U.S. has a surplus. Thus, the basis of a free market of trading commences and also involves services, including labor.

It should be remembered that the war of independence and the founding of America was in reaction to an import tax on tea which precipitated the Boston Tea Party and led to the birth of America.

The World Trade Organization (WTO) is the principle body involved in rationalizing the world's trading complexities. It is composed of 150 member states and has an affiliation with the U.N., and it is criticized for promoting the interests of the more powerful countries. Despite this criticism, the less developed countries have now secured over 30% of the world's trading volume.

Fragmented and splintered groups are all part of the organization and part of the control problem. They include:

- North American Free Trade Association (NAFTA)
- Asian Pacific Economic Cooperation (APEC)
- Free Trade Area of the Americas (FTAA)
- European Free Trade Area (EFTA) (now defunct)
- European Union (EU)

In addition, there is a whole variety of separate agreements between individual countries. One can well imagine the difficulty of coordinating, and more importantly, of keeping everybody happy. By definition, the free market system starts to fall apart when charges, i.e., tariffs, subsidies and selected exceptions, are introduced. This brings up the all important subject of financial factors.

Currencies- Setting the utopian objective of a common world currency, the Global is a far reaching dream that will eventually help to obviate the need for tariffs and other economic barriers. It is a dream, however, which is being tested with the larger countries of the European Union operating with the Euro as a common currency. When this idea was suggested, the skeptics said the logistics alone of launching the Euro were impractical. Well! In 2001 the Euro was launched virtually without incident and has been working as a common currency ever since. There was the ongoing issue of double labeling being used to pacify the older generation, but this is disappearing with time and the advent of the younger generation. The biggest problem is keeping all members working with the agreed budgeting rules relative to their gross national product.

A common world currency, the **Global**, is not an impossible dream although it will obviously take many generations for its realization.

Deficit Spending- This is an important issue relating to currency, and America is most probably the world's leading proponent of its usage. It has used the method effectively in expanding its economy, and it has contributed to the huge advancement of modern living. The general population has also been encouraged by salesmen to buy material products on the time payment basis. This, in turn, has forced GDP growth to an extremely high level. The government covers its deficit spending actions by printing more money and selling bonds to raise funds for budgets and other spending which creates various forms of national debt which eventually has to be repaid with taxes. Deficit spending is a very useful action if a crisis occurs and money is needed as a cushion to work through a difficult period. But if one uses the approach constantly, up to or beyond a sensible level, the cushion theory is destroyed. It can create unduly high national debt, the servicing of which saps tax revenues and can provide serious problems for future generations. Individuals also use deficit spending by buying products and services on time payments and using credit cards. This process was originally used with big ticket items like home mortgages. It was the only way for most people to acquire a home, and they often spent 30 years, and sometimes the rest of their lives paying off the debt. This practice has progressively spread to lesser items such as cars, and today is used for almost all living expenses. The result is that sometimes the individuals will acquire debt to an unserviceable level, and they have to forfeit the products and sometimes go into personal bankruptcy. Companies can also exceed reasonable debt levels and follow the same bankruptcy course of action. One can only say that, whether it is a country, company or individual, deficit spending is a useful tool if used sparingly, but if it is over exercised, it can ruin the operating economy of any user.

Entitlements and Benefits- 200 years ago life was considerably simpler from many points of view. There were no entitlements, benefits or health insurance, and people paid their own way or relied on family assistance .They worked hard, didn't live long and retirement had not been invented. About the only financial items an individual would become involved with was a mortgage on the house and, maybe, insurance. The few more wealthy people who owned stock or other properties usually bought them and kept the papers in a tin box for long periods of time. They might have to use a country doctor and sometimes a cottage hospital, and if these were needed they were usually paid for in cash. People tried to save money for these so called "rainy days" and other emergencies, but saving for old age was a rarity.

The industrial revolution brought with it exploitation and the need for unions which started to demand that the companies provide benefits. This commenced with wage levels and progressed to job protection, paid holidays, health insurance and retirement. These benefits only applied to the factory workers and, eventually, the governments got involved with entitlements to cover everyone for a wide range of issues. This form of benefit and entitlement expanded and progressed and had reached a very high level by the end of the twentieth century when global competition for products showed that U.S. companies were uncompetitive. This was partly because Americans were paid higher wages, but particularly because the companies were paying benefits not only for current workers but also the health insurance and pensions for retirees. This was not prevalent with the competition that just relied on their country's government entitlements.

This was particularly evident in such occupations as the American auto and airline industries where health and retirement benefits had risen to exceptionally high levels. To help prevent these companies from becoming bankrupt, the U.S. government has been compelled to provide at least some assistance of partially covering the corporate retirement payments. But, if this problem progresses much further, it could eventually bankrupt the government with its already overburdened financial obligations from deficit spending.

Language- One of the American founding fathers said that what ever America speaks will become the language of the world. This somewhat conceited remark is, however, turning out to be a well-founded fact. With the various occupations of North America, the language could have turned out to be Spanish, French or English. But, with English being spoken at the time of independence, it not only became the language of America but is also becoming the language of the world.

Before WWII the international diplomatic language was French which had been used since before Victorian times; it was even used by the Russian Court not only in Russia, but also when the Court wintered in the South of France.

Since WWII the need for selecting a world language has become more defined. Standardization of marine and aviation communications needs was imperative for convenience and safety. The final need, however, has arisen out of the computerization of all world actions and business needs where multiple languages are becoming an unnecessary burden, and there is a need for a common communications based language. The language now used in international meetings has drifted from French to English.

In some ways it is unfortunate that English was chosen as it is the language that evolved through centuries of multiple occupations of Great Britain. These included Nordic peoples, Germanic tribes and Norman speaking French with each leaving a residue of words. It is also a confusing tongue because of its differences between the written and spoken forms with the words such as knee, knave, knife, knit, know and many others which are pronounced without the "K." But for whatever reason, English is fast becoming the international language and is progressively being taught as a second language in many countries, particularly where they already have international activities. But, because of nationalistic pride, it is better left to spread naturally rather than by enforcement, except where safety is involved.

Human Resource Utilization-There is an obvious need to utilize some of the world's available resources for people to enjoy themselves when relaxing. These include all sports and entertainment activities which are not only enjoyed by people, but also serve for bonding of nations internationally which is a most important part of globalization. There are, however, some occupations which have seemingly expanded excessively and detract from the country's capability to progress and improve.

A notable example is the legal profession in America, a country which has become a litigious nation in recent years. Hardly a day passes without some minor incident becoming a major lawsuit. Such ridiculous happenings as a cleaning company being sued for millions of dollars for losing a pair of trousers can only be interpreted as frivolous and resource wasting. The old label of "ambulance chasers" has now been expanded to cover all phases of work and living with the result of using large quantities of highly intellectual manpower on these frivolous pursuits. When one looks at the ratio of lawyers to engineers in different world economies, it is interesting that those generating more engineers than lawyers are becoming the world leaders in technical developments. Excessive numbers of lawyers can create a double negative by not only absorbing large amounts of intellectual manpower, but they often self-perpetuate by generating over-protectionism for the public. Every minor incident is considered a possible law suit.

Another industry that has expanded out of all proportion is the financial advisers and the stock market trading groups. Stocks and bonds used to be a form of saving and were bought principally for the interest they paid, and if capital gains were involved, they were considered an added bonus. The documents relating to these acquisitions were usually put in tin boxes and safes and seldom looked at and even passed on to heirs. The whole picture has changed to what can only be likened to Las Vegas with changing ownerships on a frequent gambling basis and even to the extent of day trading. This has created a huge industry of non-contributing people which, again, detracts capabilities from meaningful progress and improvement activities. The only good thing you can say about it is that it has provided a hobby for many retirees who become addicted and spend many hours looking after their wealth. But, even they have to remember that for every winner, there's a loser.

The third example of detracting capabilities is what can only be labeled as political and voting activities. Some western countries have controlled this waste of labor by putting restrictions on the period of political campaigning until a very short period before an election. For example, England has limited these political activities until six weeks before a major election. Meanwhile, the uncontrolled situation in the U.S. has given birth to another whole industry which is not only continuously involved but works years ahead.

Achievement and success in the international arena is highly dependent on a country's contributing capabilities which are surely detracted from by these foregoing activities.

In summarizing these issues, one can only say that management and control systems have a great deal of opportunity to progressively improve in the future. This is true whether it applies to national or international entities, business groups or personal management issues with all their cultural and religious implications. The countries collective capabilities should be aimed at achieving a sustainable and peaceful future for the world.

Chapter 15

HUMANS-BODY AND SOUL

The most important ingredient in the resolving of world problems is the individual and collective decision making capabilities of humans. Therefore, it is appropriate to briefly analyze man as a human being, figuratively not clinically, in order to come to a conclusion of how he might influence the resolving of World Crisis issues.

Humans are wonderfully complex creatures or machines which, when reduced to basics, can be visualized as two main parts-**The body and the brain**; each is useless without the other. The body is the physical carrier of the brain but is basically totally responsive to the brain's instructions and directions, and it also sends back responsive messages for the brain's consideration.

The body is a marvelous physical machine with literally hundreds of parts and systems which operate and interrelate to the brain's commands and decisions. The body has been progressively dissected and analyzed by man who now has considerable knowledge of how it works. It has a surprising capability for endurance and an extensive ability to self-heal and repair itself. Man, however, now knows enough about the body to assist in its repair and maintenance processes, but there is still much to learn. In recent years, he has finally discovered the DNA structure and the ingredients of the genes. This will eventually enable him to start diagnosing the need for assistance instead of the largely trial and error methods that have been practiced until the present.

Humans need to gather sustenance from three essential ingredients in order to exist and flourish. They include **air (oxygen), water and food.** In addition, they need warmth, shelter and light.

The first essential element, **air** (oxygen), which is available in large quantities and is largely generated by the chemical interchange cycle of air and vegetation, is activated by the sun.

The second essential element is **water** which, fortunately, is also available in great quantities and is a virtually indestructible recyclable material. The action of the sun evaporates water from the oceans and then returns the moisture to earth in the form of rain. Its distribution on earth is sometimes erratic because of weather patterns caused by the earth's surface variations spinning around at approximately 1,000 miles per hour.

It is interesting to look at a glass of clear drinking water on the dining table and wonder if it may have passed through the kidneys of a dinosaur millions of years ago.

The third essential element is **food.** This can be provided by direct consumption of earth grown products such as fruit, vegetables, cereals, nuts, etc., or by indirect products such as meat, milk, fish and poultry. This last category allows humans to eat concentrated portions of energy bearing substances that have been developed by a host creature raised on direct or indirect sun-dependent products. Food is the basic fuel that supplies the energy to power humans through life by means of the digestive system that consumes and processes the nutritional material. This is another example of unimaginable ingenuity of the body that has the ability to run on a wide range of materials or fuels as long as they are renewable, sun-based products. The process commences with a taste mechanism that has the capability to recognize good materials from bad materials by pleasant or unpleasant taste or smell.

The food is first machinated by the teeth then swallowed and passed to the stomach where the digestion processes starts to segregate, extract and chemically prepare the food material as fuel for supplying to the various systems. The surplus, or non-wanted, portions from this process are collected and discharged by defecation. Abuses, overloading or wrongful acceptance induces vomiting or diarrhea to cleanse the system.

The body has an amazing ability to heal itself when some mishap or infliction occurs. Mankind has learned enough about the body to assist in the repair process but nature is the principal healer.

It is interesting to compare these human systems with man-made machines which are presently limited to a narrow range of fuels and have none of the selective capabilities or checks and balances of the human body and certainly do not heal themselves.

The other support necessities of warmth, shelter and light are again provided by direct or indirect actions of the sun.

Humans can survive for several weeks without food because they build reserves into their body system. However, they can only survive without water or liquids for a few days depending on the existing environmental conditions. And, finally, they can only survive for a minute or two without air (oxygen). Therefore, the quality and quantity of these three essential elements have to be protected to minimize interruptions of supply to ensure the continuation of life.

There are well over 6 billion humans, countless animals and unimaginable numbers of insects on this earth. Each one of these creatures must have its share of the essential food elements each day, and it does so by ingesting portions of the direct or indirect recyclable crops available to them. The body's internal system digests the input chemically, extracts the energy or nutrition as fuel for the body and brain and defecates the surplus. The difference in weight between the input and excrement is very small, but it is enough to provide all the energy or sustenance that a creature needs to survive and propagate. It's totally amazing how nature and man's organizational capabilities have kept reasonable pace with this monumental problem of supply and distribution of the human's food necessities, particularly with the drastic increase in the world's population.

It is important to note that all creatures in this world are totally dependent on the sun rising in the east each day and setting in the west to provide all their worldly needs. It is easy to see why early religions used the sun as the focal point for saying, "Thank you."

The human brain is relatively small, is located in the head and is protected by a scull. It has no visible moving parts but is the mental center of activity for receiving messages from the body and for sending replies and instructions. Figuratively, it contains the mind with its capability for learning and storing information. It also houses a command center with accommodation for reviewing and debating issues which is called the conscience. This is an individuals private retreat, and it gives them total seclusion for performing the very important occupation of **thinking**; it allows them to analyze, plan and debate issues with themselves which is a most useful tool in the learning process. The facility also houses an unlimited sized memory bank where all actions and records from activities and debates can be filed. It is also a place where they can commune with God in total privacy for personal prayer and other deep thinking.

This mental thinking facility, the conscience, is the all-important place where individuals make the decisions on good or bad, right or wrong, apply available logic and determine their responses and opinions to questions and issues. It, therefore, becomes the target for other people who want to influence the individual's opinion for political, religious or other reasons.

The body and brain need rest or sleep for recouping after activities. This normally happens each 24 hour period and usually occurs at night. During this sleep period many of the connections between the body and brain shutdown or are partially shut off, and the human being becomes semi-conscious. The senses of feeling, hearing and smelling still remain partially operative and will react if appropriate. The respiration and blood circulation are two other systems which keep working full time but at a slower rate. Many other systems keep active during sleep. These include digestion, heart pumping, lymph gland circulation, and, most importantly, the brain, which never completely shuts down under normal circumstances. Capability to think is governed by how much knowledge or experience it has acquired. There is also a command center of the brain called the conscience where all the deep thinking, debating and decision making take place. This is also the planning center and has an enormous capacity for knowledge; it seemingly has an unlimited memory capability.

The human brain performs a wide range of mental functions and decision making which is influenced by the level of human knowledge. It is this process that generates and controls all human actions and decisions which maybe small, big or even global. All of these factors are influenced by their level of education and learning. These knowledge aspects can be acquired by straight forward learning which, as always, is influenced by teaching capability and environmental conditions. Guiding and educating the conscience is a much more difficult equation. It not only involves the selection of good and bad and right and wrong but is influenced by the individual's emotions such as desires, love and hate and, particularly, by faith and religious beliefs. These influencing factors are also based on learning but of a very different type from the strait forward assimilation of knowledge. Experience and even history play an important part in this process, and religion has a strange and profound effect.

Like the body, the brain has the capability of repairing itself but with a very different process. An example of this is experienced by people who suffer a debilitating stroke. Strokes take various forms. One common type is when the blood flow to the brain is interrupted it can be accompanied by a clotting or embolism which can kill off segments causing paralysis, loss of speech capability or maybe sight together with other actions depending on which sections are affected. The affected area shows up on scans as a black hole where the blood clot has destroyed the segment. This is a permanent scar or injury to the brain which continues to show up indefinitely. The person suffering the attack is sometimes permanently disabled but often can develop a full or partial recovery by diligent therapy.

It is thought that the brain cannot grow new cells, so the question becomes, "What happens to repair capabilities such as balance, hand to eye coordination and a variety of other body actions?" Apparently, the brain is a very clever computer which can relocate the programming activities from the dead segment to other areas. With therapeutic practice the body can be taught to respond to the newly relocated messages from the brain. In this way, over a period of time, the individual can sometimes return to a near normal condition. It is an example of how ingenious the human brain and body systems are compared to man-made computers and machines.

Going back only a few hundred years in history, crime, barbarism and cruelty were rife. Although some of these factors are still prevalent today, they are very much subdued compared to conditions that existed in the Middle Ages. At that time it was necessary to create walled towns and villages to help prevent rape, plunder and torture by roving bands of barbarians. Over the years experience has ingrained most humans with a better choice of right and wrong and good and bad.

The subjects of mathematics and literature are based on deduced logic and facts, but the rules for the conscience are less definitive and quantifiable. However, the learning curve on such factors can also be accelerated by good demonstrations and debate. Many people have experienced lecturing and debating with infants who were intent on doing something wrong by generally accepted standards. Surprisingly enough, little kids usually intuitively know the difference between right and wrong, but their emotions and other feelings sometimes take priority during the decision-making process. Maybe Walt Disney's character of Jiminy Cricket in Pinocchio saying, "Give a little whistle and always let your conscience be your guide" was to good effect.

The list of factors and issues that influence the human brain in its decision making process is never-ending and includes the most important issues of religion and sex, each of which need individual definition and discussion.

Religion is an issue which has a profound effect on the decision-making of the brain and involves complexities which are very difficult to define, evaluate and analyze.

Religion seemingly emanates from the recognition of a spiritual being that is responsible for generating the wondrous world we live in; this spiritual being is a center for singular or collective communication through prayer to say thanks, request help and is always present to respond to one's needs through life and maybe even to whatever happens after death.

The basic documents or scriptures of many religions were spoken by the wise men of the time, passed along by word of mouth and written down by scribes, usually very much later. These writings reflected teachings and codes of living of that time by people whose knowledge of the world was limited to their basic locality and subject to their personal assignations. These documents have been interpreted and translated over the ages and have become the basis for a given religion's teachings. Although they vary greatly, they have certain basics in common- they attempt to define right from wrong and often claim the wise man heard the words directly from God. Like all man-made writings, they can be interpreted differently to serve the purpose of the beholder and his desires.

One can well imagine an illiterate peasant in ancient times asking the wise men of the day, "How was the world created?" The wise men did a great PR job of illustrating an answer in words by sectioning the events into the seven days of the week. Deeply religious people often interpret this literally because humans, then and now, cannot possibly really comprehend how the world was created. The scientists have discovered much about how the world has evolved but will acknowledge that there is a superior being or God whose overall workings he also cannot comprehend. Both the religious extremists and the scientists are correct, but it is wrong to try and supplant factual science by a spiritual belief with words from the scriptures in a world where scientific knowledge and logic is urgently needed to solve many of the world's ongoing major problems.

A person's designated religion is almost always determined at birth by which ever denomination the family happens to be. The newly born child plays no part in the choice, but whatever sect or denomination the family happens to be usually remains with the child for the rest of its life. The level of religious education the child receives from the family, visits to the holy house or school are implanted in his subconscious mind and becomes a most influential part of the right-wrong decision making process.

Some religions are racially based and often have teachings inherent in their school systems together with regulated times of prayer. The leaders of these religions are, therefore, powerful influences over the people and sometimes even become heads of state. As many of the ancient religious scriptures are open to interpretation, the religious leaders have freedom to apply their personal inputs to their interpretation which on some occasions can take a peaceful religion and turn it into a set of hateful beliefs. This all leads to a very closely knit society and often plays a huge and necessary part in some people's lives.

Comparing this strictly governed religious person to an example of today's individual from the Western world, one finds a very different type. He is very often a person who is deeply involved in enjoying living in the present world of comfort and convenience, has no particular religious affiliation and does not get involved with the church except for births, marriages or deaths or when in need of spiritual support. This lack of religious affiliation is, by far, the norm in the developed western countries, although many of these people are classified in surveys by their birth religion.

Many people who have only occasional connection with religion in their early years still have strong, sub-conscious religious influences on their decision making later in life. This becomes very important when issues arise that are considered as stand alone political subjects but are in fact part of a religious ruling. For example, the world's population is forecast to expand from 6.4 billion persons to date to 9.4 by 2050. Again, it should be noted that all this increase is estimated to be in the less developed countries where AIDS is rampant. These are the same areas where the Roman Catholic Church is gaining numbers although loosing out world wide. It is obvious that birth control is an ever increasing need and AIDS is rampant without preventative condoms. But, unfortunately, the R. C. church still stands by its impractical total "abstinence from sex" solution to the problem which is a losing battle because it is fighting human nature.

Sex. - When the almighty being, God, created man he made him in male and female forms and gave him the ability to reproduce by the act of sex. The day God issued or made the sexual parts of humans he sure wasn't stingy. He gave out portions that created feelings that would last from cradle to grave, not only for propagation but, to generate social attention and action for pleasure and excitement beyond all other feelings.

He gave little girls the feelings of thrills and shivers to wrap in silk and lace which together with their voluptuous curves provide the bait for attracting the opposite sex. Little boys were stuffed with enough hormones to shake and quiver from childhood through manhood and beyond.

The result is the attraction for pairing up in marriage and for propagation together with continuing pleasurable action that is for ever present with the sexes. This sometimes manifests itself in harmless flirting outside marriage as social enjoyment but can also sometimes develop into serious affiliations that wreck marriages and ruin careers. The conscious and the subconscious mind are hard pressed when the mind and body gears up on a proposed sexual exploit. The normal right-wrong codes, and even the religious guidance factors, get pushed aside in the sexual decision making conflict of the mind.

Another influencing set of factors are the subjects of emotions, feelings and reactions which are also very difficult to define and quantify. For each positive item there is, unfortunately, an apposing negative equivalent. For example:

- Love-Hate
- Like-Dislike
- Help-Hinder
- Smile-Frown
- Happy-Sad
- Well mannered-Ill mannered
- Reserved-Boastful, etc.

These items are reflected as body expressions and become part of a person's character and personality and are influential in how others see him.

The brain consciously or subconsciously takes all these and many more factors or issues into account when debating an action and coming to a conclusion. Logic often fights desires, and lack of patience sometimes becomes the major influencing item. Also, religious training and beliefs of faith can become the final balance of judgment. Change and improvement does happen with time, on a progressive basis and can been hastened by learning and good governance. The accelerated rate and development of social systems has brought advancement to some but accentuated the "gap" with the less fortunate. Modern, virtually instantaneous communication systems have greatly improved opportunities for implementing leveling actions, but it has also brought the "gap" into full-view of the less fortunate, which breeds hate and envy.

Abraham Lincoln's statement, "Everyman is born free and equal" was a nice thought, but in reality, it is not the case. Some are lucky and are born into families and situations that are intelligent, loving, comfortable and rich. Others are born into poverty, sickness, ignorance, hate and strife. This is not to say that all the positive and negative factors at birth are indicators of future possible happiness and achievement of an individual. Because at birth, the brain and body start developing with other influencing factors such as initiative, drive and the all important natural capabilities of the individual. In the developed world many successful people have come from humble families because their diligence to improve has taken over together with the will to achieve and succeed. However, the person born into poverty, sickness, hatred and ignorance generally has much less opportunity.

But Lincoln was right in that there should be the objective of working towards "every one being born free and equal" which should be an inherent factor in any normal World program.

There is often the hope and desire that developed countries can quickly change these important leveling factors by a few conferences and agreements. However, even with modern Electronic Communication systems, there is a limit to how much the "rate of change" can be speeded up. Therefore, the human capability of patience has to come into play. One has to recognize that, in many cases, the dividing issues will take long periods of time to resolve, sometimes outside a human life span.

A good example is the tumult and strife that presently exists in the Middle East. This whole situation will naturally change of its own accord when the "Age of Oil" comes to an end. Western nations will have less commercial reason for their presence in the region. Also, the local inhabitants will have to change their whole way of life when income from oil is diminished. The Royal rich are likely to progressively become poorer and have to start administering their countries on a real, not artificial, basis. They will have to rely on assistance from others by joining the move towards Globalization and a future peaceful existence.

Cultures- The conscious and subconscious parts of the human brain are the basis for developing cultures; they vary greatly between countries and are influenced by many factors. Of particular interest are the differences in cultural reaction, of a given country in times of major events or conflicts. For instance, the fact is that some countries, in times of war, train men to become Kamikaze pilots which is out of context to their normal quiet cultural appearance. Also, other, more hostile countries find no problem with draping men, women and children with explosives to become walking bombs.

In May of 1961, when America was in conflict on many fronts and was lagging behind in scientific development, President Kennedy made his famous speech on the Apollo program about which he said, "Before this decade is out, we will land a man on the moon," and then he continued, "...and return him safely to earth." It makes one think that some nations may have omitted the last part of the statement to greatly simplify the scientific challenge ahead.

Some governments become deeply involved with their religious faiths which influence their approach to world affairs. Over the centuries this has sometimes generated conflicts which, in turn, have led to wars. This issue is still prevalent today, and there is a great need and opportunity for world-wide religious leaders to rationalize common factors between religions to help quell conflicts instead of helping to create them.

Chapter 16

SUMMARY

Over the last 200-300 years the world has evolved to a wondrous level of comfort and convenience by changing from an agricultural to an industrialized society. This development, however, has brought with it huge problems involving the issues of **Population, Energy, Environment and Sustainability.**

Mankind is slowly starting to realize that many of the principal materials used in developing and maintaining this wondrous world are finite. That despite their apparent abundance, they are non-renewable and, consequently, non- sustaining, and their availability will cease in the course of time. They include: iron, steel, aluminum and all the other metals together with many of the chemical based elements including: coal, oil, chemical fertilizers, uranium, cement, etc.

The reason that this monumental problem has been ignored is that there is a choice between long term "Sustainability programs" which are often outside the human life span or the short term approach of "let's enjoy it while it lasts." even if it destroys the face of the earth. The public often supports this last approach and responds with, "Why should I worry because I won't be here when it happens."

However, **Oil,** one of the critical commodities in this equation, is starting to show the signs of reaching the point where demand exceeds availability. This, coupled with other events, i.e., 9/11 and the Iraq war, has caused the price of oil to increase dramatically. The oil supply problem has been exacerbated by the lack of a long term planning program and the fact there is, as yet, no agreement upon a renewable replacement material.

It is vitally important for people to start understanding that oil is now starting to run out and the only known meaningful and practical replacements are derived from sun-reared renewable crops. This is the same source from which humans and all living creatures have found their food since the inception of life on Earth. Also, all fossil and non-renewable materials will, in the course of time, progressively become exhausted, and their replacement will also have to come from earths naturally occurring cycles, i.e. solar, wind, geothermal, etc., or derived from these same recyclable crops.

Another competitor for the use of the increasingly valuable land is man's constant desirer to expand the "Concrete jungle" for his living and commercial use! For the foreseeable future there will be a constant battle between using the available land for **food, energy and space for people to live and work.**

The only way this huge competitive demand for renewable vegetation will be satisfied is to initiate a massive agricultural program and start replanting the earth and returning the world to an agricultural basis. Coincidentally, it will be necessary to progressively stop mining for non-renewable materials and control other actions that are degrading the land and prohibiting its further use for farming purposes.

As the world crisis materialized, the public started to become aware of the importance of oil and the transportation system by the high price of gasoline at the pump and the related financial implications of the market price of a barrel of crude oil. The deep recession we are now in was first triggered by 9/11 and the escalating cost of oil. This, in turn, increased the cost of living, and the implications of the price and supply of oil led to drastically slowing down the massive construction and housing industry, a high transportation user. This exposed the improprieties of the mortgage loan industry which was issuing sub-prime mortgages to doubtfully qualified customers. It also showed that the banking industry was in financial turmoil because of lack of controls and irresponsible decisions making. Installing controls now is rather like locking the barn door and watching the overpaid horsemen ride over the horizon while the barn is stacked full of toxic home loans.

While a renewable replacement for oil is vitally important to solve the transportation energy issue, its resolution will also be the starting point for a chain of events that could help solve many factors in the other major problem categories of Population and Environment.

This oil crisis, the cause of all the trouble, was, and still is, assumed by many to be a passing aberration and that the price of oil will eventually be reduced. This has already happened to a degree as world commercial activity has temporarily slowed down because of the recession, and the price of a barrel of oil has dropped. It is, however, still three times the price paid at 9/11. The cost of a barrel of oil (1 barrel = 42 gallons) has risen from $21.00 in 2001 to over $100 in 2008, although now it is reduced to about $70. This cost to the United States financial system is over $1.5 billion per day. It will also start rising again when commercial activity resumes with a further disastrous effect on the economy. People still don't believe the high price of oil is here to stay, and the problem will never get solved if people do not think that it exists.

Another related issue is that the U. S. Government, companies and the public use "deficit spending" for solving economic problems. This was a great system for developing our huge GDP when everything was on the upswing. Now, with the down turn, it is becoming a millstone around our necks. It has already caused a banking crisis because of the extensive use of sub-prime mortgages, and there are also a high number of defaults on credit cards and other personal debts. Meanwhile, the government has to print more money, to which there is a limit.

The government must become involved with the oil replacement issue with an intensity that it needs and deserves. Intensity similar to that aroused for WW II and the moon program. The first item to be resolved is the decision from which renewable material the replacement tank fuel is to be derived. When made, it will allow the automobile and fuel manufacturers to concentrate their developments in a meaningful direction. It will also start the all important actions in expanding agriculture which is the only practical source of a renewable replacement material for oil and other non-renewables.

It is also necessary for the government to become involved with the intermediate phase of oil conservation. This requires that the public become aware that the necessary fuel savings can only be attained by driving smaller, lighter and more efficient cars. To force a drastic downsizing of cars in a meaningful time span, it will be necessary to tax gasoline progressively up to a price of about $8 per gallon which is the same price paid in Europe. The price will eventually get to this level and beyond by market forces alone, but it will take a long time because the public tolerates agony applied slowly without reacting. The drastic increase in price is necessary

Summary

to create awareness and "kick start" car down-sizing. People will then clamor for smaller cars, and it could bring in revenues in the order of $ 2.5 billion per day. This will help to fill the financial void to provide funds to help meet other deficits that have been, and are continuing to, be created. Taxing gasoline is obviously not going to be popular politically, and it needs ingenuity of explanation for selling it to the public. The alternative is not doing anything meaningful and letting the country lead the world even deeper into the economic downturn which is not a popular move either. This gasoline replacement issue decision could be a most meaningful and historic action and start to regain American automotive leadership. On a positive note, the gasoline price increase will decrease the use of gasoline and the basic price of oil will drop, and that will provide more time for developing an alternative fuel.

The whole critical oil situation could have been contained a few years ago by taking the pricing action. At that time it would have been a relatively minor operation. But American politicians took the easy way out and assumed that market forces would take care of the problem. This would eventually be true of course, but by the time they are effective the issue will have grown into an incurable cancer permeating every crevice of the world's economic structure.

In the heavy truck field there is a great opportunity for conservation and saving of up to a million barrels per day with a revised design of tractors and standard trailers employing improved aerodynamics, as outlined in this book.

Up to the present, most of the government support for an oil replacement has been directed to the use of hydrogen which is academically appropriate but practically very unlikely. Hydrogen is difficult to produce from renewable resources unless you have an excess of electricity like Iceland with its naturally provided hydro and geothermal contributions. Also, hydrogen has serious unsolved problems in its handling and storage and its use in the hands of the general public. A proposal has been made that hydrogen could be generated at the site of the filling station by using natural gas to minimize storing and shipping problems. But natural gas is generated by the same decaying fossils which generate oil and, consequently, is likely to run out in a similar time span as oil. Another material that has been suggested for hydrogen production is coal. This, of cause, is another fossil material with diabolical pollution factors, and the promoters of its use are, naturally, the coal mining states who propose to catch the pollution involved and bury it. It is another case of quick exploitation for dollars and to hell with the future. Hydrogen, however, will be part of the future transportation fuel equation because it is prevalent in other materials such as methanol which can be used as a carrier and can be made from biomass and trees. But methanol would be the fuel to put in the tank, and the hydrogen would be extracted on the vehicle by a device called a reformer. Methanol is a commonly available fuel from any hardware store today marketed under the name "denatured alcohol" and has none of the storage or handling problems of raw hydrogen. It can be used with today's conventional internal combustion engines and is also a candidate for powering fuel cells which are the anticipated propulsion medium for vehicles of the future. It will, however, require an agricultural land program for growing the trees or other vegetation for biomass as will any of the renewables derived from recyclable crops. Also, there are other types of vegetation materials being researched to see whether there are more advantageous plant materials that could be used for generating a replacement for oil. Although the forthcoming transportation fuel energy crisis will be responded to with a variety of approaches, to have more than one major tank fuel for vehicles would be a logistical nightmare for distribution.

It is generally agreed that the next base fuel material is likely to be derived from renewable crops. As this is a long term item, it would be prudent for the government to start now the preliminaries of an extended agricultural program. Starting a massive program for replanting the earth's surface will require the use of land in the less developed countries and require a large labor force to enact the scheme. This will provide jobs for many uneducated people who live in this these areas and are the base cause of the population problem with its lack of family planning.

The change back from mono farming to mixed farming will obviously reduce the fuel used for food production and distribution. It will also provide the opportunity to change from the chemical based non-renewable ground preparation materials to synthetic copies of natural based products, as developed by Cuba. This will not only provide more nutritional foods, but also have less damaging by-products and, most importantly, drastically reduce the mining with its associated land degradation.

One of the worst offenders of mining degradation and atmospheric pollution is coal which today provides much of the world's production of generated electricity. It is anticipated that the continuation of sun, wind, wave and tide and particularly geothermal development will eventually replace coal's contribution to the energy pool. Nuclear energy is often proposed as a replacement for coal to generate electricity. However, although nuclear usage does not generate large quantities of undesirable pollutants, it does strip large areas of land in its mining and it also has a serious, so far unresolved disposal problem of atomic waste. It should also be noted that nuclear is derived from non-renewable uranium, and, therefore, it will have a limited lifespan. It is not renewable and consequently not sustainable.

The U.N. is the logical choice to head up this massive land reclamation exercise and maybe the whole oil replacement program. But first it has to be reformed and developed to be an honest, respected organization, planning on a long-term continuing basis and providing a forum for global debate.

Another important issue we are facing at this moment is America's reputation and what other people think of us. We used to be envied, respected, admired and appreciated for becoming involved in two world wars with military forces as a means of last resort to save diabolical situations. We were all also admired and respected for our technical feats of the moon program, the GPS satellite system and space exploration. Our auto industry was a world leader in production and much innovative advancement.

Today, as a result of our actions in recent years, we are disliked and feared by many and even hated by some. This is largely because other countries think we have abused our position as the richest country in the world with the world's mightiest military machine. But like many Americans, they think we are inappropriately getting involved in unwinable wars which get started by the whims of individuals without appropriate debate and support from other countries and the U.N... Also getting deeply involved in the Arab-Jewish conflict in Israel has not improved the situation, particularly with the associated oil issue. The fact that we have only 5% of the world's population but use 25% of the world's available oil each day, of which 70% is imported from other countries, has not endeared us to the world, particularly when we have not moved meaningfully on any oil conservation program or on the associated pollution issues. Coincidently, the U.S. auto industry, which used to be highly respected, has deteriorated from the world's leader to the brink of extinction because it has lagged way behind in designing appropriate small, fuel efficient vehicles for the depressed economic times. This is largely because it has become dominated by a "Styling and Sales" culture without the appropriate regard for function. It is going to take many years and a lot hard work for America to become a respected world leader again.

This is a dangerous period in history with China and India, with much larger populations, rapidly expanding their GDP's, military strengths and general standards of living. If we continue to antagonize other countries and peoples, it could be the turning point in U.S. world domination.

In the future it is going to be necessary for the more developed countries to realize that some realigning of the wealth distribution is an unavoidable by-product of progress and building barriers with walls or tariffs is only a temporary delay of the inevitable.

The Western World needs to progressively modernize its governmental systems to ensure only qualified participants are involved and cease interfering in other countries cultures and stop trying to force on them the present form of democracy or alternative religions.

It is hoped religions throughout the world will start interrelating and find common ground in order to quell conflicts and facilitate education for the less developed countries and help in controlling the population explosion.

If these factors can be realized and responded to, the world will return to a sustainable and continuing basis.

It is also hoped that this book will help the reader to start thinking and planning beyond their life span.

POSTSCRIPT

As we continue to traverse the quagmire that's been created by the world crisis, one can only be thankful that we now have a President at the helm who is smart enough, strong enough and brave enough to take on the whole spectrum of issues at one time. This is necessary because the programs involved have situations and solutions that are interrelated; also, the slide into deeper recession has happened so quickly that it did not permit a program of selectively solving issues one by one.

One should be able to come to this conclusion by honest review regardless of one's skin color, Democrat or Republican affiliation, capitalist or communist leanings, CEO or blue collar worker status or Christian, Jew, Muslim or other national or religious segmentation. In his short time in office the new President has managed to launch actions on the multi-front of programs including domestic and international issues. He's done this despite the negatives of our political system which allow the opposition parties' continued political actions and distractions to prevail while they prepare for the next election.

Unfortunately, at the same time, we also have to acknowledge that our whole governmental, social and business systems had been called into question and need total review and consideration. It has become clear that we can't blindly trust individuals, corporations or governmental systems to do the honest and right thing without appropriate fool-proof checks and balances.

To continue to assert or assume leadership because of having the highest GDP wealth or level of military force are serious misnomers. They only results in further conflict.

Under the circumstances continuing to promote our great capitalist free market approach with its democratic system has a hollow ring about it. We need to work toward a new political system which will include elements of socialism and religious faith, and once the election is over, everybody must pull in the same direction until the next political conflict is due.

Change has never been more appropriate or necessary.

Writing in about 1800 A.D., Dickens commenced his book A Tale of Two Cities with the statement:

> *It was the best of times, it was the worst of times, it was the age of wisdom, it was the age of foolishness, it was the epoch of belief, it was the epoch of incredulity, it was a season of light, it was a season of darkness, it was spring of hope, it was the winter of despair, we had everything before us, we had nothing before us, we were all going direct to heaven, we were all going direct the other way'---*

It's amazing how his words are still appropriate today.

LaVergne, TN USA
05 December 2009

166064LV00004B/1/P